BUILT IN THE CLOUD

Azure for New Developers

FIRST EDITION

Preface

Cloud computing has revolutionized the way we build, deploy, and scale applications. As organizations continue to transition from traditional on-premises infrastructures to cloud-based environments, the demand for developers who understand cloud-native development practices has grown exponentially. This book is designed to equip new and aspiring developers with a practical, hands-on understanding of cloud computing, particularly within the Microsoft Azure ecosystem.

From foundational concepts to real-world scenarios, this first edition covers the complete cloud development lifecycle. Beginning with a comprehensive introduction to cloud computing, it then delves into the core services offered by Azure, resource management strategies, deployment pipelines, data services, and security considerations. You'll also explore advanced topics like scaling applications, optimizing performance, and managing cloud costs effectively.

The structure of the book follows a logical progression. Chapters 1 and 2 introduce the fundamentals of cloud computing and Azure. Chapters 3 through 6 focus on core development, deployment, and data management tasks. Chapter 7 addresses monitoring and security, while Chapter 8 dives into performance and scalability best practices. Chapter 9 provides real-world examples that connect the concepts and services discussed in earlier chapters. Finally, Chapter 10 outlines your path forward with certifications, community involvement, and further learning.

Whether you are new to cloud development or transitioning from another platform, this book aims to serve as a foundational guide. By the end of this book, you should feel confident in your ability to build, deploy, and manage applications on Azure, and be well-equipped to explore its more advanced capabilities.

Welcome to your journey in cloud development—let's get started!

Table of Contents

Chapter 1: Getting Started with Cloud Computing

Understanding Cloud Computing Concepts

Cloud computing has transformed the landscape of software development by introducing a paradigm shift in how applications are built, deployed, and scaled. Rather than relying on physical hardware and static infrastructure, developers can now use cloud platforms to provision, manage, and scale resources dynamically. But what is cloud computing at its core, and why has it become so fundamental to modern software development?

Cloud computing is the on-demand delivery of IT resources—like computing power, storage, databases, networking, software, analytics, and intelligence—over the internet with pay-as-you-go pricing. Instead of buying, owning, and maintaining physical data centers and servers, organizations can acquire technology services such as servers, storage, and databases on an as-needed basis from cloud providers like Microsoft Azure, Amazon Web Services (AWS), and Google Cloud Platform (GCP).

The Evolution of Cloud Computing

To understand the significance of cloud computing, it's helpful to examine its evolution. Traditionally, businesses operated on a capital expenditure (CapEx) model, investing heavily in hardware and software, data centers, and IT personnel. This approach often led to underutilized resources, slow scaling, and high maintenance costs.

Cloud computing shifted this to an operational expenditure (OpEx) model. Resources could now be rented based on usage, freeing organizations from the overhead of infrastructure management and enabling rapid scalability and innovation.

Essential Characteristics of Cloud Computing

Cloud computing is defined by five key characteristics, as outlined by the National Institute of Standards and Technology (NIST):

1. **On-Demand Self-Service**: Users can provision computing capabilities as needed without human interaction with each service provider.

2. **Broad Network Access**: Services are available over the network and accessed through standard mechanisms, promoting use on various platforms.

3. **Resource Pooling**: Provider resources are pooled to serve multiple consumers using a multi-tenant model, with different physical and virtual resources dynamically assigned.

4. **Rapid Elasticity**: Capabilities can be elastically provisioned and released to scale rapidly outward and inward.

5. **Measured Service**: Resource usage is monitored, controlled, and reported for transparency and optimization.

Deployment Models of Cloud Computing

Cloud computing can be deployed in several models, depending on organizational needs:

- **Public Cloud**: Services are delivered over the public internet and shared across organizations. Microsoft Azure is a public cloud provider.

- **Private Cloud**: Dedicated infrastructure operated solely for a single organization, either on-premises or hosted.

- **Hybrid Cloud**: A mix of public and private cloud infrastructures that remain distinct but are interconnected for greater flexibility.

- **Multi-Cloud**: Utilizing multiple cloud providers for different services or tasks.

Each model has its benefits and trade-offs. Public clouds offer cost efficiency and scalability. Private clouds provide greater control and security. Hybrid and multi-cloud approaches balance these aspects.

Service Models: IaaS, PaaS, SaaS

Cloud services are categorized into three main models:

- **Infrastructure as a Service (IaaS)**: Provides virtualized computing resources over the internet. Users manage OS, apps, and storage while the provider handles networking and physical hardware. Azure Virtual Machines are a prime example.

- **Platform as a Service (PaaS)**: Offers a platform allowing customers to develop, run, and manage applications without dealing with infrastructure. Azure App Services is a PaaS offering.

- **Software as a Service (SaaS)**: Delivers software over the internet, eliminating the need for installations. Microsoft 365 and Azure DevOps fall into this category.

Understanding these models helps developers determine the level of control they need over their environment and the trade-offs in flexibility versus simplicity.

Benefits of Cloud Development

Modern software development thrives in cloud environments due to several benefits:

1. **Scalability**: Cloud platforms can scale resources up or down automatically based on demand.

2. **Cost Efficiency**: The pay-as-you-go model ensures you only pay for what you use.

3. **Performance Optimization**: Global infrastructure ensures low latency and high availability.

4. **Security and Compliance**: Enterprise-grade security and compliance features are built into major platforms.

5. **Rapid Deployment**: Developers can provision and deploy services quickly, enhancing productivity.

6. **Innovation**: Access to emerging technologies like AI, ML, and IoT empowers developers to innovate without building complex infrastructure.

Challenges of Cloud Computing

Despite its advantages, cloud computing also presents challenges:

- **Vendor Lock-In**: Relying heavily on one provider can make it difficult to migrate to another platform.

- **Data Security and Privacy**: Cloud providers implement security measures, but ultimate responsibility for data protection lies with the user.

- **Downtime and Reliability**: Although rare, outages can affect application availability.

- **Cost Management**: Without proper monitoring, costs can spiral due to underutilized or forgotten resources.

Azure's Position in the Cloud Landscape

Microsoft Azure is one of the leading cloud service providers, offering a vast array of services tailored for developers, enterprises, and startups. Its integration with Microsoft tools (like Visual Studio, GitHub, and Power Platform), hybrid capabilities, and strong enterprise presence make it an attractive choice for .NET developers and organizations with Microsoft-based ecosystems.

Azure is particularly strong in:

- Hybrid cloud deployments

- Enterprise-grade security and compliance

- Developer productivity tools

- Artificial Intelligence and Machine Learning services

- Integration with DevOps pipelines and automation tools

The Role of Developers in Cloud Computing

As a developer, your responsibilities in the cloud shift compared to traditional development. You're no longer limited to writing code—you also make decisions about deployment environments, scaling strategies, cost optimizations, and security configurations.

Here are some new responsibilities you might encounter:

- Writing **infrastructure-as-code** (IaC) scripts using tools like ARM templates or Bicep

- Automating deployment pipelines with **CI/CD**

- Integrating cloud-native services like **serverless functions**, **event-driven workflows**, or **managed databases**

- Monitoring application performance using tools like **Azure Monitor** and **Application Insights**

Practical Example: Setting Up a Simple Web App

To illustrate a basic cloud computing task, here's how you might set up a simple web app using Azure App Service (PaaS):

```
# Login to Azure CLI
az login

# Create a resource group
az group create --name myResourceGroup --location "East US"

# Create an App Service plan
az appservice plan create --name myAppServicePlan --resource-group
myResourceGroup --sku FREE

# Create a Web App
az webapp create --name myUniqueAppName123 --resource-group
myResourceGroup --plan myAppServicePlan
```

```
# Deploy a sample app (assuming you have a local repo set up)
az webapp deployment source config-local-git --name
myUniqueAppName123 --resource-group myResourceGroup
```

This simple workflow shows how infrastructure and app hosting can be managed entirely through command-line tools in a matter of minutes—something unthinkable in traditional server environments.

Looking Ahead

Understanding cloud computing concepts is the essential first step in your journey. In the next sections, we'll explore the tangible benefits of cloud development, dig deeper into service models, and introduce you to the tools and terminology you'll encounter on the Azure platform. By the end of Chapter 1, you'll have a solid theoretical and practical foundation to begin working with Microsoft Azure confidently.

Benefits of Cloud Development

Cloud development offers a transformative approach to software creation and deployment. It empowers developers and organizations to innovate rapidly, deploy efficiently, and operate at scale—without the traditional burdens of maintaining infrastructure. This section provides a deep dive into the benefits of cloud development from the perspective of agility, scalability, performance, collaboration, security, and cost.

Agility and Speed to Market

One of the primary drivers of cloud adoption is the dramatic increase in development and deployment speed. Traditional IT operations require significant setup time, including hardware procurement, installation, and software configuration. In contrast, cloud development allows provisioning of complete environments within minutes.

Using services like **Azure Resource Manager (ARM)** templates or **Bicep**, developers can define infrastructure as code and replicate environments effortlessly across development, staging, and production:

```
resource webApp 'Microsoft.Web/sites@2021-02-01' = {
  name: 'my-web-app'
  location: resourceGroup().location
  kind: 'app'
  properties: {
    serverFarmId: appServicePlan.id
  }
}
```

This kind of automation drastically reduces the time required to get applications into the hands of users. Furthermore, developers can rapidly iterate and deploy updates using tools like **GitHub Actions** or **Azure Pipelines**, leading to shorter release cycles and faster feature delivery.

Scalability and Elastic Resource Management

Cloud platforms like Azure provide virtually unlimited resources that can be scaled dynamically based on real-time demand. This elasticity is particularly beneficial for applications with variable traffic patterns. For example, an e-commerce site may experience spikes during seasonal sales; rather than manually provisioning servers in advance, auto-scaling rules can be configured.

In Azure App Service, autoscale can be configured based on a variety of metrics:

- CPU utilization

- Memory usage

- Request count

- Custom metrics via Azure Monitor

Example JSON for setting autoscale rules:

```json
{
  "autoscaleSettings": {
    "profiles": [
      {
        "name": "AutoScaleProfile",
        "capacity": {
          "minimum": "1",
          "maximum": "10",
          "default": "2"
        },
        "rules": [
          {
            "metricTrigger": {
              "metricName": "CpuPercentage",
              "operator": "GreaterThan",
              "threshold": 70,
              "direction": "Increase",
              "statistic": "Average",
              "timeGrain": "PT1M",
```

```
                "timeWindow": "PT5M",
                "timeAggregation": "Average"
            },
            "scaleAction": {
                "direction": "Increase",
                "type": "ChangeCount",
                "value": "1",
                "cooldown": "PT5M"
            }
        }
    ]
}
]
}
}
```

With the cloud, developers no longer need to estimate hardware requirements up front, which leads to more efficient resource utilization and greater reliability under load.

Reliability and High Availability

Azure's global infrastructure is designed for fault tolerance and high availability. Developers can deploy applications across multiple **regions**, **availability zones**, and **data centers**, ensuring redundancy and disaster recovery.

Azure's **Traffic Manager** and **Load Balancer** services allow distribution of traffic across regions and instances, which can automatically failover in case of an outage. This ensures minimal disruption to end users.

For example, a multi-region deployment can be configured with:

- Primary region: East US

- Secondary region: West Europe

- Automatic failover via Traffic Manager

This setup supports business continuity and meets stringent uptime requirements (99.99%+ SLAs in many services).

Enhanced Developer Productivity

Cloud development environments provide a wealth of tools and services that streamline the entire development lifecycle. Features like:

- **Azure DevOps**: Full CI/CD pipelines, work tracking, and testing

- **Visual Studio Code and Azure Extensions**: Direct deployment and management from your IDE

- **Azure Functions**: Quick creation of serverless APIs with minimal configuration

- **GitHub Codespaces**: Spin up full dev environments in the cloud in seconds

These tools remove friction from traditional development, allowing developers to focus on writing code rather than managing infrastructure. For example, an entire CI/CD pipeline can be created via a few clicks in Azure DevOps, integrating repositories, builds, tests, and releases.

Cost Optimization

One of the most significant advantages of cloud development is cost efficiency. Instead of large capital expenditures (CapEx) for infrastructure, organizations pay only for what they use—a consumption-based pricing model (OpEx).

Developers and teams can leverage:

- **Reserved instances** for predictable workloads (discounted pricing)

- **Spot instances** for low-priority jobs (massive cost savings)

- **Autoscaling** to eliminate underutilized resources

- **Cost analysis and budgeting** tools in Azure to monitor and forecast expenses

Azure's **Cost Management + Billing** service provides actionable insights. For example, if a development VM runs 24/7 but is only needed during working hours, automation can shut it down during off-hours.

```
# Auto shutdown a VM daily at 7PM
az vm auto-shutdown --resource-group DevRG --name DevVM --time 1900
--email dev@myorg.com
```

This level of control can reduce waste and maximize ROI.

Built-in Security and Compliance

Cloud platforms come with robust, enterprise-grade security mechanisms by default. Azure, for example, has over 90 compliance offerings, including GDPR, ISO, SOC, and HIPAA. Developers can benefit from:

- **Role-Based Access Control (RBAC)** for fine-grained permissions

- **Azure Security Center** for threat detection and vulnerability scanning

- **Private endpoints and VNets** for secure service-to-service communication

- **Key Vault** for secure storage of secrets, certificates, and API keys

In a cloud-native approach, security is not an afterthought. Infrastructure-as-code ensures security configurations are version-controlled and consistently applied. Alerts and automated responses can be set up for incidents, and integration with tools like **Microsoft Defender for Cloud** helps secure the full stack.

Continuous Integration and Continuous Deployment (CI/CD)

Cloud development encourages and facilitates the adoption of CI/CD practices. These practices help teams integrate code more frequently, run automated tests, and deploy to production with confidence.

Using Azure Pipelines or GitHub Actions, developers can define automated workflows:

```
# GitHub Actions example for deploying to Azure App Service
name: Deploy to Azure
on:
  push:
    branches:
      - main
jobs:
  build-and-deploy:
    runs-on: ubuntu-latest
    steps:
      - uses: actions/checkout@v2
      - name: Setup Node
        uses: actions/setup-node@v3
        with:
          node-version: '18.x'
      - run: npm install
      - run: npm run build
      - uses: azure/webapps-deploy@v2
        with:
          app-name: 'my-web-app'
          publish-profile: ${{ secrets.AZURE_WEBAPP_PUBLISH_PROFILE
}}
          package: .
```

These pipelines reduce manual deployment errors and increase the quality and stability of releases. Developers gain confidence that changes can be shipped rapidly and safely.

Dev-Test and Experimentation Environments

Cloud services support ephemeral environments for experimentation and QA. Teams can create entire stacks for testing, run automated integration tests, and tear them down automatically after use. This flexibility supports innovation without affecting production environments.

Azure also offers **sandbox environments** for learning and trial runs, as well as **developer pricing tiers** for most services.

Example: A QA engineer can create a full replica of production using a script, validate a new feature, and remove the environment within an hour—incurring minimal cost.

Global Reach and Localization

Applications hosted in the cloud can be deployed close to end users using global data centers, reducing latency and improving user experience. Azure's **Content Delivery Network (CDN)** and **Traffic Manager** optimize content delivery and routing based on user location.

With cloud-native services, developers can support:

- Multilingual applications with Azure Cognitive Services

- Geographically distributed databases like Cosmos DB

- Compliance with data residency laws

This global reach enables even small startups to operate at an international level with minimal overhead.

Ecosystem and Integration

The Azure ecosystem is rich with integration points, enabling developers to build complex, feature-rich systems. Services such as:

- **Azure Logic Apps**: For workflow orchestration and business process automation

- **Azure Event Grid and Service Bus**: For event-driven architectures

- **Azure API Management**: For publishing and managing APIs

- **Power Platform**: For building low-code/no-code apps and automations

This vast ecosystem allows developers to choose the right tools for each task and integrate seamlessly with other Microsoft or third-party platforms.

Developer Empowerment and Innovation

Cloud development shifts the power dynamic. Developers can independently provision environments, experiment, and deploy with minimal friction. This autonomy accelerates innovation and reduces dependency on operations teams.

The combination of cloud-native architectures (like microservices, containers, and serverless), automation (via IaC and CI/CD), and platform services (like AI/ML, analytics, and messaging) creates a rich canvas for innovation.

Whether building a real-time chat app, a large-scale data processing pipeline, or a machine-learning powered recommendation engine, the cloud provides everything needed—from idea to deployment.

Summary

The benefits of cloud development are vast and transformative. They include:

- Rapid development and deployment

- Seamless scalability

- Global reach

- Enhanced security

- Cost savings and efficiency

- Empowered developers

By embracing the cloud, organizations unlock new possibilities, improve operational agility, and accelerate innovation. The cloud is not just a hosting solution—it's a fundamental enabler of modern software development. As we continue through this book, you'll explore how to apply these principles using Microsoft Azure, one of the most powerful and developer-friendly cloud platforms available today.

Overview of Cloud Service Models: IaaS, PaaS, SaaS

Cloud computing offers a flexible stack of services that vary in the level of abstraction and control. These services are typically divided into three primary models: Infrastructure as a Service (IaaS), Platform as a Service (PaaS), and Software as a Service (SaaS). Each model represents a different layer of the computing stack, and understanding them is critical for making informed architectural and operational decisions when building and deploying applications in the cloud.

This section explores each of these models in depth, using Microsoft Azure as the reference platform. You will learn about their core features, use cases, advantages, and trade-offs. Additionally, we will compare them side-by-side to help clarify which model fits best in various development scenarios.

Understanding the Cloud Stack

Before diving into each model, it helps to visualize them as a spectrum of responsibility:

- **IaaS**: You manage the operating system, runtime, data, and applications. The cloud provider manages the virtualization, servers, storage, and networking.

- **PaaS**: You manage applications and data. The cloud provider manages everything else, including OS, middleware, and runtime.

- **SaaS**: The cloud provider delivers fully managed software. You simply use the application.

Here's a simplified chart of responsibility:

Stack Component	On-Premises	IaaS	PaaS	SaaS
Applications	You	You	You	Vendor
Data	You	You	You	Vendor
Runtime	You	You	Vendor	Vendor
Middleware	You	You	Vendor	Vendor
OS	You	You	Vendor	Vendor
Virtualization	You	Vendor	Vendor	Vendor
Servers	You	Vendor	Vendor	Vendor
Storage	You	Vendor	Vendor	Vendor

Infrastructure as a Service (IaaS)

IaaS is the most flexible cloud computing model. It provides virtualized hardware resources over the internet, allowing users to build and manage their own infrastructure without purchasing physical machines.

Azure offers IaaS through services such as:

- **Azure Virtual Machines (VMs)**

- **Azure Virtual Network (VNet)**

- **Azure Load Balancer**

- **Azure Storage**

Key Features

- Full control over OS and installed software

- Customizable networking and security configurations

- Pay-as-you-go pricing for compute, storage, and bandwidth

- Rapid provisioning and scaling of virtualized resources

Common Use Cases

- Hosting legacy applications

- Creating dev/test environments

- Running custom workloads or third-party applications

- Migrating on-premises systems to the cloud

Example: Creating a VM with Azure CLI

```
az vm create \
  --name myVM \
  --resource-group myResourceGroup \
  --image UbuntuLTS \
  --admin-username azureuser \
```

```
--generate-ssh-keys
```

This command provisions a Linux VM using the default Azure image, a common first step for IaaS-based development.

Advantages

- High level of control and flexibility

- Broad compatibility with existing workloads

- Easy lift-and-shift from on-premises infrastructure

Trade-offs

- Requires more management effort

- User is responsible for patching and updates

- Complex architecture decisions (e.g., scaling, redundancy)

Platform as a Service (PaaS)

PaaS provides a development and deployment environment in the cloud, abstracting away infrastructure concerns. It enables developers to focus on building applications without managing servers, storage, or networking.

Azure's key PaaS offerings include:

- **Azure App Service**

- **Azure Functions**

- **Azure SQL Database**

- **Azure Logic Apps**

- **Azure Kubernetes Service (AKS)** (hybrid between IaaS and PaaS)

Key Features

- Managed runtime environments

- Integrated development tools and deployment workflows

- Auto-scaling and load balancing

- Built-in security, patching, and monitoring

Common Use Cases

- Web and API applications

- Microservices architectures

- Serverless applications

- Continuous integration and delivery pipelines

Example: Deploying a Web App with Azure App Service

```
az webapp up --name myWebApp --resource-group myResourceGroup --
location "Central US"
```

This single command pushes your application to the cloud, provisions the required resources, and sets up a managed hosting environment.

Advantages

- Faster development and deployment

- Reduced operational overhead

- Built-in scaling, monitoring, and integration

- Focus on application logic and business value

Trade-offs

- Less control over the underlying infrastructure

- Limited customization compared to IaaS

- Possible vendor lock-in due to proprietary features

Software as a Service (SaaS)

SaaS is a software delivery model in which applications are hosted by a cloud provider and accessed by users over the internet. The provider manages everything, from infrastructure to data and application updates.

Azure offers SaaS solutions such as:

- **Microsoft 365**

- **Power BI**

- **Dynamics 365**

- **Azure DevOps Services**

Key Features

- Turnkey software solutions

- Access via web or APIs

- Subscription-based pricing

- Always up-to-date and secure

Common Use Cases

- Email, collaboration, and productivity tools

- CRM and ERP systems

- Business intelligence and analytics

- Developer productivity tools (e.g., Git repos, CI/CD)

Example: Integrating SaaS with APIs

Even though you don't deploy SaaS software yourself, Azure often enables integration through APIs. For example, you might use Power BI's REST API to embed dashboards into your application:

```
GET https://api.powerbi.com/v1.0/myorg/reports
Authorization: Bearer <access_token>
```

Advantages

- No infrastructure or maintenance overhead

- Immediate access to features and updates

- Ideal for end-user applications

Trade-offs

- Limited customization

- Vendor controls update cycle

- Data governance may be complex for sensitive workloads

Comparing IaaS, PaaS, and SaaS

Feature	IaaS	PaaS	SaaS
Developer Control	Full control	Code and config only	None (consumer-level usage)
Management Overhead	High	Medium	Low
Customization	Maximum	Moderate	Minimal
Time to Market	Slow	Fast	Instant
Ideal For	Legacy apps, custom VMs	Web apps, APIs, microservices	Productivity, analytics

When to Use Each Model

Choosing the right model depends on your project's requirements:

- **Use IaaS when:**

    - You need full control over the OS and environment

    - You are migrating legacy systems

    - You require custom hardware configurations

- **Use PaaS when:**

    - You want to focus on application code

- You are developing modern web or mobile apps

- You need rapid deployment and auto-scaling

- **Use SaaS** when:

  - You want out-of-the-box software functionality

  - You're looking for quick productivity gains

  - You don't want to manage infrastructure or applications

Hybrid and Evolving Models

In practice, many solutions use a mix of IaaS, PaaS, and SaaS. For instance:

- A company might run a legacy ERP system on VMs (IaaS),

- Host its customer-facing app via App Service (PaaS),

- And use Power BI for internal reporting (SaaS).

Additionally, modern cloud offerings increasingly blur these lines. Azure Kubernetes Service, for example, provides managed infrastructure (PaaS-like), but also gives full control over container orchestration (IaaS-like).

Future Directions

As cloud computing evolves, more abstractions and integrations are being introduced:

- **Function as a Service (FaaS)**: Complete abstraction of infrastructure for event-driven computing (e.g., Azure Functions).

- **Container as a Service (CaaS)**: Managed container orchestration with tools like AKS.

- **Backend as a Service (BaaS)**: Pre-built backend services for authentication, databases, and messaging (e.g., Firebase, Azure Mobile Apps).

These emerging models continue to simplify development while expanding capabilities.

Summary

Understanding the cloud service models is foundational to leveraging the cloud effectively. Each model—Infrastructure as a Service (IaaS), Platform as a Service (PaaS), and Software as a Service (SaaS)—offers unique advantages and is suited to different scenarios.

- **IaaS** provides the most control and flexibility but requires more management.

- **PaaS** offers a balanced environment for rapid development and deployment with reduced operational burden.

- **SaaS** delivers complete software solutions with zero infrastructure responsibilities.

By selecting the right combination of models, developers and organizations can optimize their cloud strategy, balancing customization, agility, scalability, and cost. The next section will explore the key terminology and concepts that underpin the Azure platform, helping you navigate and utilize it with confidence.

Key Terminology and Concepts for Azure

To effectively develop in Microsoft Azure, it's essential to understand the terminology and foundational concepts that underpin the platform. Azure provides a vast ecosystem of services, tools, and abstractions, each playing a specific role in modern cloud computing. This section offers an in-depth explanation of these core concepts, enabling you to navigate the Azure environment with confidence and precision.

Azure Subscription

An **Azure subscription** is the logical container that holds all the resources you create in Azure. It's tied to a billing account and is used to manage access, resources, and costs. Every Azure account can have multiple subscriptions, each with its own isolated resources and billing.

Use cases for multiple subscriptions include:

- Separating environments (e.g., Development, QA, Production)

- Department-level cost tracking

- Role-based access delegation

```
# List all subscriptions
az account list --output table

# Set a specific subscription as active
az account set --subscription "MySubscriptionName"
```

Each subscription has a unique **Subscription ID**, and this ID is often required when deploying resources via CLI, scripts, or templates.

Resource Group

A **Resource Group** is a container that holds related resources for an Azure solution. It provides a way to manage and organize resources that share the same lifecycle, such as a web app, database, and storage account.

Resource Groups support:

- Role-based access control (RBAC)

- Tagging and cost management

- Consolidated monitoring and alerts

```
# Create a resource group
az group create --name myResourceGroup --location "East US"
```

Deleting a resource group deletes all resources within it—this is useful for cleaning up entire environments quickly.

Azure Regions and Availability Zones

Azure is a globally distributed platform with data centers located in regions around the world. An **Azure Region** is a geographical area (e.g., West Europe, East US) where Azure services are hosted.

Regions may contain **Availability Zones**, which are physically separate data centers within the same region. These zones help build highly available applications by distributing workloads across multiple locations.

For example, to improve fault tolerance, you could deploy your application across three zones in East US 2.

Some services are **region-specific** (e.g., Azure App Service), while others are **globally available** (e.g., Azure Active Directory).

```
# List available regions
az account list-locations --output table
```

Azure Resource Manager (ARM)

Azure Resource Manager (ARM) is the deployment and management service for Azure. It enables you to create, update, and delete resources in your Azure account using declarative templates, known as ARM templates.

ARM provides:

- Resource grouping and tagging

- Dependency management

- Consistent deployment across environments

Example ARM Template snippet to deploy an App Service:

```
{
  "type": "Microsoft.Web/sites",
  "apiVersion": "2021-02-01",
  "name": "myWebApp",
  "location": "East US",
  "properties": {
    "serverFarmId": "[resourceId('Microsoft.Web/serverfarms',
'myAppServicePlan')]"
  }
}
```

You can also use **Bicep**, a simpler DSL (Domain Specific Language) that compiles into ARM templates.

Azure Services

Azure services are grouped into categories based on their functionality:

- **Compute**: Virtual Machines, App Services, Functions

- **Storage**: Blob Storage, Table Storage, Disk Storage

- **Networking**: Virtual Network, Load Balancer, VPN Gateway

- **Databases**: Azure SQL, Cosmos DB, MySQL, PostgreSQL

- **AI and Machine Learning**: Cognitive Services, Azure Machine Learning

- **DevOps**: Azure DevOps, GitHub Actions

- **Security**: Azure Security Center, Azure Key Vault, Azure Sentinel

Each service is delivered via REST APIs, SDKs, and the Azure Portal, and can be provisioned via CLI, ARM, Bicep, or Terraform.

Azure App Service

App Service is a fully managed platform for building web apps, RESTful APIs, and mobile backends. It supports multiple programming languages including .NET, Java, Node.js, Python, and PHP.

Features include:

- Autoscaling and load balancing

- Deployment slots

- Built-in CI/CD

- Integration with Azure DevOps and GitHub

```
# Create an App Service plan and web app
az appservice plan create --name myPlan --resource-group
myResourceGroup --sku B1 --is-linux
az webapp create --name myWebApp --resource-group myResourceGroup --
plan myPlan --runtime "NODE|18-lts"
```

Azure Functions

Azure Functions is Azure's serverless compute offering that allows you to run small pieces of code (functions) without managing infrastructure. Functions are triggered by events such as HTTP requests, messages in a queue, or a timer.

Benefits include:

- Pay-per-execution pricing

- Automatic scaling

- Event-driven architecture

Example function (JavaScript):

```
module.exports = async function (context, req) {
```

```
    context.res = {
        body: "Hello, Azure!"
    };
};
```

Functions can be deployed via CLI, VS Code, or GitHub Actions.

Azure Storage

Azure provides several types of storage to meet diverse application needs:

- **Blob Storage**: Unstructured object storage for text, media, backups

- **Table Storage**: NoSQL key-value data store

- **Queue Storage**: Messaging between components

- **File Storage**: SMB-based file shares

Blob Storage example (CLI):

```
az storage account create --name mystorageacct --resource-group
myResourceGroup --location eastus --sku Standard_LRS
az storage container create --account-name mystorageacct --name
mycontainer --public-access blob
```

These services are highly durable (99.999999999% availability) and are commonly used for media storage, logs, backups, and large file uploads.

Azure Identity and Access Management (IAM)

Azure uses **Azure Active Directory (Azure AD)** for authentication and authorization. Key components of identity management in Azure include:

- **Users and Groups**: Managed identities for people and services

- **Service Principals**: Non-human identities used by apps and automation

- **Role-Based Access Control (RBAC)**: Fine-grained access control

Example: Assign Reader role to a user on a resource group:

```
az role assignment create \
  --assignee user@example.com \
```

```
--role Reader \
--resource-group myResourceGroup
```

Azure also supports **Managed Identities** to authenticate securely to services without storing secrets.

Azure Monitor and Application Insights

Monitoring and diagnostics are critical for modern applications. Azure provides comprehensive observability tools:

- **Azure Monitor**: Metrics, logs, alerts for all Azure resources

- **Application Insights**: Deep performance insights for applications

Use cases include:

- Real-time alerting

- Telemetry collection

- Application tracing

- Dashboarding and analytics

Example query in Application Insights Analytics:

```
requests
| where timestamp > ago(1h)
| summarize count() by resultCode
```

Azure Marketplace and Templates

The **Azure Marketplace** provides a catalog of pre-built solutions, virtual machines, applications, and templates from Microsoft and third parties.

You can deploy solutions like:

- WordPress on Linux

- Jenkins on Ubuntu

- SQL Server on Windows Server

These solutions can be automated through **ARM templates**, enabling consistent deployments.

Azure Tags and Cost Management

Tags are name/value pairs assigned to resources to organize them for cost management and governance. For example, tagging by environment or department:

```
az tag create --name "Environment" --value "Production"
```

Azure Cost Management tools allow tracking costs across subscriptions, creating budgets, and analyzing usage patterns.

Azure CLI and PowerShell

Azure supports automation via:

- **Azure CLI**: Cross-platform, scriptable tool for managing Azure resources
- **Azure PowerShell**: Powerful for Windows admins and automation

Both tools can manage the full lifecycle of Azure services and integrate with CI/CD pipelines.

CLI example to list running VMs:

```
az vm list --show-details --query "[?powerState=='VM running']" --output table
```

PowerShell example:

```
Get-AzVM | Where-Object {$_.PowerState -eq "VM running"}
```

Azure Policy and Governance

Azure Policy allows you to enforce rules on your resources. For example, you can deny VMs in certain regions or require tags on all resources.

Example: Enforce a policy to require tags:

```
{
  "if": {
    "field": "tags",
    "exists": "false"
  },
```

```
    "then": {
      "effect": "deny"
    }
}
```

These policies help maintain compliance and governance across enterprise environments.

Summary

Understanding Azure's key terminology and concepts is essential for successful cloud development. In this section, we've covered foundational components including:

- Subscriptions and resource groups

- Regions and availability zones

- The Azure Resource Manager model

- Core services such as App Services, Storage, and Functions

- Security via RBAC and Azure AD

- Monitoring, identity, tagging, and automation

As you continue through this book, these concepts will form the bedrock of everything you build. Familiarity with these terms will ensure you can work confidently across Azure tools, templates, and workflows, and structure your cloud projects for success.

Chapter 2: Introduction to Microsoft Azure

What is Azure?

Microsoft Azure is a comprehensive cloud computing platform developed and maintained by Microsoft. It provides a wide range of cloud services—including compute, analytics, storage, networking, and AI—that enable developers, IT professionals, and businesses to build, deploy, and manage applications through Microsoft's global network of data centers. Azure offers both Platform as a Service (PaaS) and Infrastructure as a Service (IaaS) models and supports a variety of programming languages, tools, and frameworks, including both Microsoft-specific and third-party systems.

Azure is more than just a hosting environment. It's a vast ecosystem that includes hundreds of services integrated with DevOps tools, AI and machine learning capabilities, container orchestration, and hybrid cloud support. Whether you're a solo developer building a small app or a global enterprise deploying mission-critical solutions, Azure provides the tools and scale needed to support your initiatives.

History and Evolution of Azure

Azure was first announced in 2008 and launched in 2010 as "Windows Azure." It initially focused on PaaS offerings but quickly expanded into IaaS and broader services. In 2014, Microsoft rebranded the platform as "Microsoft Azure" to reflect its cross-platform, language-agnostic capabilities. Since then, it has become one of the top three public cloud platforms alongside Amazon Web Services (AWS) and Google Cloud Platform (GCP).

Azure's growth has been driven by key factors:

- Deep integration with Windows Server and enterprise tools

- Hybrid cloud support with Azure Arc and Azure Stack

- Broad global data center presence

- Comprehensive identity and security services

- A commitment to open-source tools and frameworks

As of today, Azure offers over 200 services and is used by 95% of Fortune 500 companies.

Core Principles of Azure

To understand Azure, it's essential to grasp the principles upon which it is built:

- **Elasticity**: Scale resources up or down automatically as needed.

- **High Availability**: Build applications that remain available even when individual components fail.

- **Resilience**: Handle failure gracefully through redundancy and failover mechanisms.

- **Security**: Use advanced threat protection, encryption, identity management, and compliance.

- **Global Reach**: Deploy applications across the globe with minimal latency.

These principles influence the design of every Azure service, making it a robust choice for mission-critical applications.

Azure Service Categories

Azure services are organized into logical categories to help developers and organizations select the right tools:

1. **Compute**: Azure Virtual Machines, App Services, Azure Functions

2. **Networking**: Virtual Network, Load Balancer, Application Gateway

3. **Storage**: Blob, File, Queue, and Table Storage

4. **Databases**: Azure SQL Database, Cosmos DB, Azure Database for PostgreSQL/MySQL

5. **AI and Machine Learning**: Cognitive Services, Azure ML

6. **Analytics**: Azure Synapse, HDInsight, Data Lake

7. **Security and Identity**: Azure Active Directory, Key Vault, Sentinel

8. **DevOps**: Azure DevOps, GitHub Actions, ARM Templates

9. **Containers**: Azure Kubernetes Service, Container Instances

10. **Migration**: Azure Migrate, Database Migration Service

11. **IoT**: IoT Hub, Azure Sphere

12. **Hybrid**: Azure Arc, Azure Stack

These categories make Azure versatile and suitable for a wide range of workloads and industries.

Advantages of Using Azure

Microsoft Azure provides numerous benefits, particularly when compared with traditional infrastructure or even some competing cloud platforms:

- **Integration with Microsoft Tools**: Seamless integration with Visual Studio, GitHub, Active Directory, Power Platform, and Office 365.

- **Enterprise Readiness**: Trusted by major organizations, with robust compliance offerings (GDPR, HIPAA, ISO).

- **Hybrid Support**: Azure Stack and Azure Arc allow for hybrid cloud scenarios, blending on-prem and cloud.

- **AI and ML**: Pre-trained models and a fully managed ML platform lower the barrier for adopting AI.

- **Cost Control**: Tools like Azure Cost Management help forecast and control spending effectively.

- **Global Reach**: With data centers in over 60 regions, Azure allows apps to be deployed close to users.

How Azure Works

Azure operates on a cloud abstraction model, providing resources to users through a collection of services. These resources are allocated from physical data centers managed by Microsoft, but exposed through virtualized interfaces via the Azure Portal, Azure CLI, SDKs, REST APIs, or PowerShell.

Here's a high-level breakdown of how typical Azure workflows operate:

1. **Provisioning**: You define what you need (e.g., a web app or database) via code or UI.

2. **Deployment**: Azure allocates physical or virtual resources to fulfill your request.

3. **Management**: You monitor, scale, secure, and manage the resources through built-in or custom tools.

4. **Billing**: Azure tracks usage metrics and generates billing based on consumption.

Azure Account and Tenancy

To use Azure, you need an Azure account linked to a Microsoft identity. Within Azure, your account operates under a **tenant**, which is essentially a dedicated and trusted instance of Azure Active Directory. Inside a tenant, you manage:

- **Users and groups**

- **Subscriptions**

- **Service principals and managed identities**

- **Resource access and RBAC policies**

This structure allows organizations to segregate concerns, manage large teams, and secure workloads effectively.

Deployment Models and Abstractions

Azure supports multiple ways to deploy and manage resources:

- **Azure Portal**: A graphical web interface for provisioning and managing services.

- **Azure CLI**: Command-line interface ideal for automation and scripting.

- **Azure PowerShell**: Windows-oriented command shell with Azure modules.

- **ARM Templates**: JSON-based templates to declare resource configurations.

- **Bicep**: A simplified DSL for ARM templates.

- **Terraform**: Open-source IaC tool supported by Azure.

Example: Provisioning a web app using Bicep:

```
resource app 'Microsoft.Web/sites@2021-02-01' = {
  name: 'myApp'
  location: resourceGroup().location
  properties: {
    serverFarmId: 'myAppServicePlan'
    siteConfig: {
      appSettings: [
        {
          name: 'WEBSITE_RUN_FROM_PACKAGE'
          value: '1'
        }
      ]
```

```
      }
   }
}
```

Integration with DevOps

Azure integrates tightly with modern DevOps tools and practices:

- Use **Azure Pipelines** or **GitHub Actions** for CI/CD

- Define infrastructure using code

- Monitor deployments and rollbacks using **Application Insights**

- Host private container registries with **Azure Container Registry**

- Deploy to Kubernetes via **Azure Kubernetes Service (AKS)**

This tight integration helps teams build, test, and ship features faster and more reliably.

Azure Global Infrastructure

Azure's infrastructure spans a massive global network. It includes:

- **Regions**: Physical locations with data centers (e.g., UK South, West US 3)

- **Availability Zones**: Isolated data centers within a region

- **Edge Zones**: For ultra-low latency apps

- **Content Delivery Network (CDN)**: For fast static asset delivery

Developers can design high-availability and disaster-tolerant applications by using these layers strategically.

Use Cases for Azure

Azure supports a wide range of use cases:

- **Web and Mobile Apps**: Rapid deployment with scaling and monitoring

- **Enterprise Applications**: Integrate with legacy systems and Microsoft services

- **AI-Powered Apps**: Use prebuilt models or train your own

- **IoT Applications**: Connect, monitor, and manage devices at scale

- **Big Data Processing**: Real-time and batch analytics pipelines

- **Gaming and Media**: Host game backends or media streaming services

Pricing and Cost Models

Azure follows a **pay-as-you-go** pricing model, but also supports:

- **Reserved Instances**: Commit to usage for 1-3 years for discounts

- **Spot Instances**: Deeply discounted pricing for interruptible workloads

- **Consumption Plans**: For serverless functions and logic apps

Use the **Azure Pricing Calculator** and **Cost Management + Billing** tools to estimate and optimize your expenses.

Example: Estimating the cost of a Standard B1 App Service:

- 1 core, 1.75 GB RAM

- ~ $13/month USD (price varies by region and usage)

Summary

Microsoft Azure is a powerful and flexible cloud platform that empowers developers and organizations to build applications faster, more securely, and at scale. Its broad range of services, developer-friendly tools, and global infrastructure make it suitable for everything from personal projects to enterprise-grade applications.

In this section, we explored:

- What Azure is and how it evolved

- Its key principles and architectural structure

- The main service categories and how they align with different needs

- Deployment models, automation tools, and DevOps integration

- Use cases, pricing strategies, and global reach

As we move forward, you will begin to interact directly with the platform, starting with setting up your own Azure account and exploring the portal in detail. This hands-on experience will form the foundation for everything else you build in the cloud.

Azure's Global Infrastructure and Services

Microsoft Azure is built upon one of the largest, most secure, and most reliable cloud infrastructures in the world. This infrastructure spans the globe, supporting millions of users and enterprises with low-latency access, regional compliance, and redundancy. Azure's global infrastructure is designed to deliver high availability, data durability, and fault tolerance while maintaining top-tier performance.

This section explores Azure's physical and logical infrastructure, including regions, availability zones, edge locations, service architecture, networking backbone, and global compliance. By understanding these components, you'll be better equipped to design scalable, resilient, and globally distributed applications.

Azure Regions

An **Azure region** is a set of data centers deployed within a specific geographic location. Each region is paired with another region within the same geography to support regional disaster recovery and redundancy.

As of this writing, Azure has more than **60+ announced regions** around the world, making it one of the largest global footprints among public cloud providers. Each region is designed to support:

- Redundancy and fault isolation

- Data residency and sovereignty

- Regulatory compliance

Examples of Azure regions:

- East US

- West Europe

- Southeast Asia

- Australia East

- UK South

- Brazil South

- Central India

Azure regions are further categorized as:

- **Geographies**: Continent-level groupings (e.g., North America, Europe, Asia)

- **Sovereign Clouds**: Specialized clouds (e.g., Azure Government, Azure China, Azure Germany) with additional compliance requirements

- **Region Pairs**: Predefined regional pairs for disaster recovery (e.g., East US paired with West US)

You can list available regions using Azure CLI:

```
az account list-locations --output table
```

Availability Zones

Availability Zones (AZs) are unique physical locations within an Azure region. Each zone is made up of one or more data centers equipped with independent power, cooling, and networking. Zones are physically separated and provide high availability through redundancy.

Regions with Availability Zones support **zone-redundant services (ZRS)**. For example:

- Deploying VMs across zones protects against data center-level failure.

- Azure SQL Database can be configured with zone-redundant high availability.

- Azure Kubernetes Service (AKS) can run across zones for fault tolerance.

A typical architecture might deploy three VMs, each in a different AZ:

```
az vm create --resource-group myRG --name vm-zone1 --zone 1 ...
az vm create --resource-group myRG --name vm-zone2 --zone 2 ...
az vm create --resource-group myRG --name vm-zone3 --zone 3 ...
```

This configuration ensures the application remains operational even if one entire zone fails.

Region Pairing and Disaster Recovery

Azure automatically pairs each region with another in the same geography. These **region pairs** are used for:

- Data replication (e.g., in geo-redundant storage)

- Automated failover during large-scale outages

- Planned updates staggered between regions

Benefits of region pairing:

- Reduced likelihood of simultaneous failures

- Geo-redundant storage replication across pairs

- Faster disaster recovery scenarios

Example region pairs:

- North Europe and West Europe

- East US and West US

- Southeast Asia and East Asia

In case of a regional outage, services like Azure Site Recovery can fail over workloads to the paired region.

Edge Zones and CDN

Azure's infrastructure includes **Edge Zones** and a **Content Delivery Network (CDN)** to improve latency and performance for users globally.

- **Edge Zones**: Bring Azure services closer to end users for ultra-low latency, especially important in IoT, gaming, and real-time communication.

- **CDN**: Caches static content (images, CSS, JavaScript, media) at edge locations around the world to deliver it faster to users.

Azure CDN configuration is simple and integrates seamlessly with Azure Blob Storage and App Services:

```
az cdn profile create --name myCDNProfile --resource-group myRG --
sku Standard_Microsoft
az cdn endpoint create --name myCDNEndpoint --profile-name
myCDNProfile --resource-group myRG --origin myapp.azurewebsites.net
```

Global Network and Backbone

Azure is backed by a **global private backbone network** that connects all Azure regions and services. This network includes:

- Over 175,000 miles of fiber-optic cabling

- Private peering with major ISPs

- Dedicated connections through **Azure ExpressRoute**

- Low-latency inter-region communication

This backbone is used to route traffic securely and efficiently between services and regions, bypassing the public internet. For example:

- Data replication across regions is performed over Azure's private network

- Internal service calls (e.g., from App Service to SQL Database) benefit from high-speed links

For enterprise workloads, **ExpressRoute** offers dedicated private connectivity between your on-premises network and Azure:

```
# ExpressRoute setup is usually managed via Azure Portal or via
networking service providers
```

Azure Services and Geolocation

Not all Azure services are available in every region. This is due to factors like demand, compliance, latency, and infrastructure capability. To check if a service is available in your region:

```
az vm list-skus --location "East US" --output table
```

Services may be:

- **Global**: Available everywhere (e.g., Azure AD, Azure DNS)

- **Regional**: Available in specific data centers (e.g., App Services, VMs)

- **Zonal**: Can be deployed within a specific Availability Zone

When architecting a solution, it is essential to plan for:

- Regional availability of required services

- Redundancy across zones or regions

- Latency between services and users

Data Residency and Compliance

Azure provides tools and configurations to help meet data sovereignty and residency requirements:

- Choose regions based on local regulations (e.g., Germany North for German customers)

- Use services that offer **geo-redundancy** or **customer-managed keys**

- Enable **compliance features** like Azure Policy and Blueprints

Azure offers more than 100 compliance certifications, including:

- ISO/IEC 27001

- SOC 1, 2, and 3

- HIPAA

- GDPR

- FedRAMP (for Azure Government)

You can generate compliance reports and audit logs from **Azure Compliance Manager**.

Service-Level Agreements (SLAs)

Azure's services are backed by **SLAs** that guarantee uptime and performance:

- 99.95% for most single-instance services

- 99.99% for services deployed across Availability Zones

- Financially backed compensation if SLAs are not met

Example:

- Azure Virtual Machines SLA: 99.9% uptime for single VM, 99.95% for VMs in an availability set, 99.99% for VMs across zones

Understanding these SLAs is crucial when designing enterprise-grade systems that require high availability.

Best Practices for Using Global Infrastructure

To build resilient and efficient applications using Azure's global infrastructure:

- **Design for failure**: Use Availability Zones and region pairs

- **Minimize latency**: Deploy services near end users

- **Use caching**: Azure CDN for static content, Redis Cache for dynamic content

- **Monitor health**: Azure Monitor and Application Insights

- **Automate disaster recovery**: Use Azure Site Recovery and geo-redundant storage

- **Optimize cost**: Use local vs. global deployment where appropriate

Here's a typical multi-region architecture pattern:

- **Primary region**: Full deployment (App, DB, Cache, etc.)

- **Secondary region**: Read replicas, warm standby

- **Traffic Manager**: Routes users based on latency or geographic rules

- **Storage**: Geo-redundant (GZRS) to replicate data automatically

Summary

Azure's global infrastructure is a foundational element that enables scalable, resilient, and high-performance applications. With over 60 regions, multi-zone support, edge locations, and a high-speed private backbone, Azure is built to handle the demands of modern digital services on a global scale.

In this section, we examined:

- Azure regions and regional pairs

- Availability Zones and fault tolerance

- Edge locations, CDN, and ExpressRoute

- Regional service availability and compliance

- Design patterns for global and highly available applications

Understanding and leveraging Azure's infrastructure allows you to architect solutions that are not only powerful but also resilient and globally optimized. In the next section, we'll walk through setting up your own Azure account so you can begin deploying resources in this global cloud platform.

Setting Up an Azure Account

To begin using Microsoft Azure and take advantage of its powerful cloud computing capabilities, the first step is to set up an Azure account. Creating an account gives you access to the Azure portal, CLI, SDKs, and hundreds of services ranging from virtual machines and app services to databases and AI tools.

This section will guide you through the entire process of setting up a new Azure account, verifying your identity, understanding account structure, exploring subscription models, applying best practices, and preparing your environment for development.

Creating a Microsoft Azure Account

1. **Visit the Azure Website**

To get started, go to the official Azure website:

https://azure.microsoft.com

2. **Click "Start Free"**

Microsoft offers a free tier to new users that includes:

- $200 credit for the first 30 days

- 12 months of popular free services (like VMs, databases, and storage)

- 25+ services always free (e.g., Azure Functions, Cosmos DB with limited throughput)

Click the **"Start free"** button on the homepage to begin registration.

3. **Sign in or Create a Microsoft Account**

You'll need a Microsoft account to use Azure. If you already have one (e.g., for Outlook, Xbox, or Office 365), you can use that. Otherwise, follow the prompts to create a new one.

4. **Verify Identity**

Azure requires identity verification through:

- **Phone number**: SMS or voice call verification

- **Credit/Debit card**: Used for identity validation only; you won't be charged unless you upgrade

Important: Microsoft enforces a strict policy of not charging during the free trial period unless explicitly authorized.

5. **Review Terms and Complete Signup**

Accept the Microsoft Azure agreement, offer terms, and privacy statement. Once your identity is confirmed, you'll be redirected to the **Azure Portal**, where you can begin using your account.

Understanding the Azure Free Tier

Microsoft Azure provides a generous free tier that helps developers and businesses test out services before committing to paid plans.

Free for 12 months:

- B1S VM: Windows/Linux virtual machines (750 hours/month)

- Azure SQL Database: 250GB storage

- Azure Blob Storage: 5GB LRS hot block

- Bandwidth: 15GB egress

Always Free:

- Azure Functions: 1 million requests/month

- Event Grid: 100,000 operations/month

- Cosmos DB: 400 RU/s and 5GB storage

- Azure DevOps: 5 users per organization

$200 Credit (first 30 days):

- Use on any paid services like AKS, App Service, Cognitive Services, etc.

Use this credit strategically to try out scalable workloads or advanced services.

Azure Account Structure

Your Azure identity and billing are organized into a hierarchy that supports flexibility and scalability.

1. **Azure Account**: The top-level entity tied to a Microsoft identity.

2. **Directory (Tenant)**: Represents a dedicated Azure Active Directory instance. Tenants control user access, security policies, and identity configurations.

3. **Subscription**: A billing container for Azure services. Each subscription is associated with a tenant.

4. **Resource Group**: A logical container for related Azure resources (VMs, apps, databases).

5. **Resources**: Actual instances of services (e.g., App Services, SQL Databases).

This structure enables scenarios like:

- Isolated dev/test/production environments

- Departmental billing

- Multi-tenant SaaS applications

- Centralized identity management

Choosing a Subscription Type

Azure offers several subscription options depending on your use case:

- **Free Trial**: New users only, includes $200 credit.

- **Pay-As-You-Go**: No upfront cost; pay only for usage.

- **Microsoft Customer Agreement**: Suitable for businesses and enterprises.

- **Enterprise Agreement (EA)**: Volume licensing and long-term pricing contracts.

- **Student Account**: Free credits and services for verified students.

You can view your subscriptions with:

```
az account list --output table
```

And switch between them with:

```
az account set --subscription "My Subscription Name"
```

Setting Up Azure CLI

After account creation, it's useful to set up the Azure CLI for scripting and automation.

Install Azure CLI

For Windows:

```
Invoke-WebRequest -Uri https://aka.ms/installazurecliwindows -
OutFile .\AzureCLI.msi; Start-Process msiexec.exe -Wait -
ArgumentList '/I AzureCLI.msi /quiet'
```

For macOS:

```
brew update && brew install azure-cli
```

For Linux (Ubuntu):

```
curl -sL https://aka.ms/InstallAzureCLIDeb | sudo bash
```

Sign In to Azure CLI

```
az login
```

This command opens a browser window where you can authenticate with your Microsoft credentials. Once authenticated, you'll see a list of active subscriptions and tenant IDs.

Setting Up Your First Resource Group

Resource Groups are the starting point for organizing services in Azure.

```
az group create --name myResourceGroup --location "East US"
```

This group can now hold VMs, databases, web apps, and other resources.

To delete a resource group and everything inside it:

```
az group delete --name myResourceGroup --yes --no-wait
```

Setting Up Azure in Visual Studio Code

Visual Studio Code (VS Code) offers excellent Azure integration through extensions.

1. Install the **Azure Account** extension.

2. Install **Azure App Service**, **Azure Functions**, and **Azure Resources** extensions for deployment and resource browsing.

3. Sign in via the Azure extension pane.

4. Access and manage your subscriptions, resource groups, and services directly from the editor.

With the Azure CLI and VS Code extensions, you can fully script deployments and interact with Azure from your development environment.

Adding Team Members to Your Subscription

To collaborate with a team, you can grant role-based access to your subscription:

```
az role assignment create \
  --assignee user@example.com \
  --role Contributor \
  --scope /subscriptions/{subscription-id}
```

You can also assign roles via the Azure Portal by navigating to:

Azure Portal > Subscriptions > [Your Subscription] > Access Control (IAM)

Roles include:

- **Owner**: Full access

- **Contributor**: Manage resources, no access to billing

- **Reader**: View only

Billing and Cost Management Setup

After setting up your account, configure alerts and budgets to manage your spending:

```
az consumption budget create \
  --amount 100 \
  --category cost \
  --name "MonthlyBudget" \
  --resource-group myResourceGroup \
  --time-grain monthly \
  --start-date 2024-01-01 \
  --end-date 2024-12-31
```

Set up email alerts for when you reach certain thresholds (e.g., 80% of your budget).

Azure Portal also provides a **Cost Analysis** dashboard where you can view usage, forecasts, and set quotas.

Security Considerations

From the beginning, enforce good security practices:

- Enable **Multi-Factor Authentication (MFA)** for all users

- Use **Azure AD Roles** instead of generic user credentials

- Store secrets in **Azure Key Vault**

- Set up **Azure Policy** to enforce compliance (e.g., all resources must have tags)

Create a Key Vault:

```
az keyvault create --name myKeyVault --resource-group
myResourceGroup --location "East US"
```

Add a secret:

```
az keyvault secret set --vault-name myKeyVault --name "DbPassword" --value "MySecureP@ssword123"
```

Summary

Setting up an Azure account is your gateway to exploring cloud development on one of the world's most powerful platforms. In this section, you learned how to:

- Register and verify your Azure account

- Understand subscription models and account hierarchy

- Set up the Azure CLI and VS Code integration

- Create and manage resource groups

- Add team members with appropriate roles

- Monitor and control spending

- Apply basic security best practices

With your account now ready, you are fully equipped to start provisioning services, deploying applications, and exploring the vast capabilities of Microsoft Azure. The next step is to become familiar with the Azure Portal—the central interface where much of your cloud management takes place.

Navigating the Azure Portal

The Azure Portal is the central web-based interface for managing all aspects of your Azure services and resources. It provides a unified experience that enables users to build, deploy, monitor, and scale applications and infrastructure with ease. Whether you're deploying a virtual machine, monitoring your app's health, or setting access policies, the Azure Portal brings powerful cloud management features into a user-friendly graphical environment.

This section explores the structure and capabilities of the Azure Portal, guiding you through its core navigation elements, essential features, customizations, resource management workflows, and best practices for efficient usage.

Accessing the Azure Portal

The Azure Portal can be accessed through any modern web browser by navigating to:

https://portal.azure.com

Once logged in with your Microsoft account, you are presented with the **Dashboard**, which serves as the launching point for all operations in Azure.

You can bookmark the portal or pin it to your browser's toolbar for quick access during development.

The Dashboard

The **Dashboard** is the default landing page after you log in. It displays customizable tiles with quick access to your most-used services, resources, and metrics.

Key features:

- **Custom Dashboards**: Create and manage multiple dashboards to reflect different projects or team roles.

- **Tiles**: Add charts, resource shortcuts, service status indicators, and query results.

- **Drag-and-Drop**: Rearrange tiles for a personalized layout.

- **Shareability**: Dashboards can be private or shared across teams.

To create a new dashboard:

1. Click **Dashboard** from the left menu.

2. Select **+ New Dashboard**.

3. Use the **Tile Gallery** to add resources and metrics.

4. Save and optionally share the dashboard.

The Navigation Menu

On the left side of the portal is the **Navigation Menu**, which provides quick access to:

- **Home**: Returns to the main dashboard.

- **All Services**: View and search all available Azure services.

- **Resource Groups**: Manage logical groupings of resources.

- **Subscriptions**: View billing and usage data per subscription.

- **Virtual Machines**, **Storage Accounts**, **App Services**, etc.: Direct links to commonly used services.

You can **pin** any of these sections to your dashboard or customize the menu for faster access.

To find a service quickly, use the search bar at the top of the menu.

The Global Search Bar

Located at the top center of the portal, the **Global Search Bar** allows you to find:

- Azure services

- Resource groups and individual resources

- Documentation

- Marketplace items

- Settings and policy configurations

Example: Typing "App Services" will instantly bring up links to App Service instances and the App Services overview page.

The search feature supports filters and fuzzy matching, which makes it extremely efficient when managing large environments.

Resource Overview Pages

Clicking on any resource (e.g., a VM or storage account) brings you to its **Overview Page**, which displays:

- **Essential metrics** (CPU, memory, usage)

- **Configuration settings**

- **Monitoring charts**

- **Networking information**

- **Management options** (start/stop, scale, restart, delete)

For instance, when viewing a virtual machine, you can perform actions such as:

- Start, stop, restart, and resize

- Access through SSH or RDP

- Attach disks

- View logs and performance metrics

This page is the central control panel for managing each individual resource.

Creating Resources via the Portal

To provision a new resource:

1. Click **Create a resource** in the upper-left or on the homepage.

2. Choose a service from the categories or use the search bar.

3. Fill out the configuration form (name, region, resource group, pricing tier).

4. Review and create the resource.

For example, to create a Linux VM:

- Navigate to **Create a resource > Compute > Virtual Machine**.

- Select Ubuntu Server from the image list.

- Configure admin username, SSH key, VM size, and region.

- Assign the VM to a new or existing resource group.

- Review and click **Create**.

You can also automate this process with ARM templates, which the portal allows you to export after manual deployment.

Azure Marketplace

The **Azure Marketplace** provides pre-built solutions from Microsoft and third parties, including:

- WordPress

- Jenkins

- Docker container images

- SAP and Oracle software

- Development stacks like LAMP, MEAN, and Django

You can deploy Marketplace resources directly from the portal, streamlining the setup process.

Navigate to **Create a resource > Marketplace** to explore available solutions. Each listing includes pricing, documentation, and deployment wizards.

Monitoring and Metrics

Azure Portal includes powerful monitoring capabilities via:

- **Metrics**: Built-in graphs for key performance indicators.

- **Logs**: Integration with Azure Monitor and Log Analytics.

- **Alerts**: Trigger actions based on performance thresholds.

To monitor a resource:

1. Go to the resource's overview page.

2. Click **Monitoring > Metrics**.

3. Choose a metric (e.g., CPU usage, memory, request count).

4. Customize charts or pin them to your dashboard.

Create alerts by navigating to:

Monitoring > Alerts > + New Alert Rule

Specify:

- **Scope**: Resource to monitor

- **Condition**: Metric and threshold (e.g., CPU > 80%)

- **Action Group**: Email, webhook, automation runbook

- **Severity level** and **description**

Activity Log

The **Activity Log** tracks all control-plane operations on your Azure resources—who did what, and when. It's essential for auditing and troubleshooting.

Access via:

Monitor > Activity Log

You can filter by:

- Date

- Event type

- Resource group

- User

- Status

Example: If a VM was deleted unexpectedly, use the Activity Log to identify the initiating user and time of deletion.

Identity and Access Management (IAM)

Managing permissions is crucial in a collaborative Azure environment. IAM in the portal lets you:

- Assign roles to users and groups

- Define custom roles

- Review access to specific resources

Navigate to a resource or resource group, then:

Access Control (IAM) > Role assignments > + Add

Choose:

- **Role**: Reader, Contributor, Owner, or custom

- **Assignee**: Azure AD user, group, or service principal

This enforces **least privilege access**, a key security best practice.

Tagging and Resource Organization

Tags are key-value pairs assigned to resources to enable organization, filtering, and cost management.

Examples:

- Environment = Production

- Department = Marketing

- Owner = JohnDoe

To assign tags:

1. Navigate to a resource.

2. Click **Tags > Edit**.

3. Add or modify tag keys and values.

Tags can also be managed in bulk from the **Tag Explorer** in the portal.

Cost Management and Budgets

Track usage and control spending directly within the portal.

Navigate to:

Cost Management + Billing > Cost analysis

Features include:

- Cost breakdown by resource group, service, or region

- Budget creation with alerts

- Forecasting future usage

- Recommendations for savings

To create a budget:

1. Go to **Budgets > + Add**

2. Set scope, amount, and time range

3. Define alert thresholds and email recipients

Service Health and Notifications

Azure provides a **Service Health Dashboard** showing the status of Azure services globally and in your selected regions.

Navigate to:

Monitor > Service Health

Features:

- View active and past incidents

- Set up service health alerts

- Track planned maintenance and security advisories

Set alerts to be notified when your region experiences issues:

Service Health > Alerts > + Add

Choose:

- Services and regions to monitor

- Notification channels (email, SMS, webhook)

Portal Customization Tips

- **Theme**: Switch between light, dark, and high-contrast modes.

- **Favorites**: Pin frequently used services to the sidebar.

- **Keyboard Shortcuts**: Press G + / to search, G + D to go to Dashboard.

- **Notifications**: Bell icon alerts you to events like deployment completions and warnings.

These features help you tailor the portal to your workflow and increase productivity.

Summary

The Azure Portal is a comprehensive tool for managing cloud services in an intuitive, visual way. From provisioning and monitoring to access control and cost tracking, it covers the full lifecycle of your Azure resources.

In this section, you explored:

- The dashboard and navigation menu

- Creating and managing resources

- Accessing logs, metrics, and service health

- Managing roles, tags, and budgets

- Customizing the portal for efficiency

Mastering the Azure Portal will significantly enhance your ability to develop, deploy, and manage cloud solutions with precision and speed. With your account set up and the portal at your command, you're ready to begin deploying real applications using Azure's powerful suite of development tools and services.

Chapter 3: Core Azure Services for Developers

Azure App Services

Azure App Services is a fully managed platform for building, deploying, and scaling web applications. It is one of the most popular services among developers because it abstracts away the underlying infrastructure, allowing them to focus on writing code and building features. With built-in support for multiple programming languages, integration with development tools, and support for both Linux and Windows environments, Azure App Services offers the flexibility and power necessary for modern application development.

Overview of Azure App Services

At its core, Azure App Services provides a Platform-as-a-Service (PaaS) environment for hosting web applications, RESTful APIs, and mobile backends. It supports languages such as .NET, .NET Core, Java, Ruby, Node.js, PHP, and Python. Developers can deploy code directly from popular repositories like GitHub, Azure DevOps, or use FTP and local Git repositories.

Azure App Services also includes several key features:

- Auto-scaling and load balancing

- Integrated development and deployment pipelines

- Built-in authentication and authorization

- Custom domain and SSL support

- Staging environments for testing in production-like conditions

- Easy integration with Azure DevOps and GitHub Actions

These capabilities make it a great choice for both startups and enterprise applications, offering productivity with reduced operational complexity.

Creating Your First Azure App Service

To create an App Service, you can use the Azure Portal, Azure CLI, PowerShell, or Infrastructure as Code tools like ARM templates or Bicep. Here's an example of how to create a basic App Service using the Azure CLI:

```
# Log in to Azure
```

```
az login

# Create a resource group
az group create --name MyResourceGroup --location eastus

# Create an App Service plan
az appservice plan create --name MyAppServicePlan --resource-group
MyResourceGroup --sku B1 --is-linux

# Create a web app
az webapp create --resource-group MyResourceGroup --plan
MyAppServicePlan --name myuniquewebapp123 --runtime "NODE|18-lts"
```

This script creates a Linux-based App Service plan using the B1 pricing tier and then deploys a Node.js 18 LTS web app named `myuniquewebapp123`.

Deploying Applications to Azure App Services

Once your App Service is set up, deploying your application can be done in several ways:

- **Manual Deployment via Zip Upload:** You can upload your application as a ZIP file using the Azure Portal or CLI.

- **CI/CD Pipelines:** Configure pipelines with Azure DevOps or GitHub Actions for continuous integration and deployment.

- **Local Git Repository:** Set up a Git repository within your App Service and push directly to it.

- **FTP or FTPS:** You can use traditional FTP tools for deployment, which is useful for simple static websites or legacy apps.

Example of a GitHub Actions workflow for deploying a Node.js app:

```
name: Deploy Node.js App to Azure Web App

on:
  push:
    branches:
      - main

jobs:
  build-and-deploy:
```

```
    runs-on: ubuntu-latest
    steps:
    - name: Checkout Code
      uses: actions/checkout@v2

    - name: Set up Node.js
      uses: actions/setup-node@v3
      with:
        node-version: '18'

    - name: Install Dependencies
      run: npm install

    - name: Build
      run: npm run build

    - name: Deploy to Azure Web App
      uses: azure/webapps-deploy@v2
      with:
        app-name: 'myuniquewebapp123'
        slot-name: 'production'
        publish-profile: ${{ secrets.AZURE_WEBAPP_PUBLISH_PROFILE }}
        package: .
```

Configuration and Application Settings

Azure App Services allows you to configure a range of settings without changing your code. These settings include application variables, connection strings, and framework-specific settings.

You can manage these settings from the Azure Portal under the "Configuration" tab or use the CLI:

```
az webapp config appsettings set --resource-group MyResourceGroup --name myuniquewebapp123 --settings "APP_ENV=production"
```

This command sets the APP_ENV environment variable to "production" for your web app.

Authentication and Authorization

App Services come with built-in authentication and authorization, enabling you to integrate identity providers such as Microsoft, Google, Facebook, Twitter, and any OpenID Connect-compliant provider without writing custom code.

To enable authentication:

1. Go to the Azure Portal.

2. Select your App Service.

3. Navigate to **Authentication** under the **Settings** section.

4. Click **Add identity provider** and choose your preferred provider.

5. Provide necessary credentials and configuration.

This allows you to secure your application endpoints with minimal development effort.

Custom Domains and SSL

You can bind a custom domain to your App Service. This is essential for branding and SEO purposes. To do so:

1. Purchase a domain or use an existing one.

2. Add a custom domain in the App Service's **Custom domains** section.

3. Verify domain ownership using TXT or CNAME records.

4. Bind the domain to the app.

5. Add an SSL certificate, either from Azure or a third-party provider.

Azure also offers free App Service Managed Certificates for secure HTTPS connections.

Scaling and Performance

Azure App Services supports both manual and automatic scaling, which is critical for handling varying traffic loads.

Manual Scaling

You can manually increase the instance count or scale up to a higher pricing tier via the Portal or CLI.

Autoscaling

Define rules based on metrics like CPU usage, memory usage, or request count to automatically scale up/down.

Example autoscale rule (via CLI):

```
az monitor autoscale rule create \
  --resource-group MyResourceGroup \
  --autoscale-name myAutoScaleSettings \
  --condition "CpuPercentage > 70 avg 5m" \
  --scale out 1
```

This rule adds an instance if average CPU usage exceeds 70% over 5 minutes.

Staging Environments and Deployment Slots

Azure App Services supports deployment slots, which allow you to create staging environments for testing changes before swapping them into production.

Benefits of deployment slots:

- Zero-downtime deployments

- Easy rollback if needed

- Separation of environments for testing, QA, and production

Example:

- Create a staging slot: myuniquewebapp123-staging

- Deploy to the slot

- Test your application

- Swap the slot with production

This way, your production users are never exposed to potential breaking changes during deployment.

Logging and Diagnostics

App Services provides rich logging and diagnostic capabilities, which are essential for troubleshooting and performance monitoring.

Types of logs:

- **Application logs** (code-level logs)

- **Web server logs** (IIS/Apache/Nginx logs)

- **Detailed error messages**

- **Failed request tracing**

You can enable these logs from the Azure Portal or CLI:

```
az webapp log config --name myuniquewebapp123 --resource-group
MyResourceGroup --application-logging filesystem
```

Logs can be streamed in real-time:

```
az webapp log tail --name myuniquewebapp123 --resource-group
MyResourceGroup
```

Integration with Other Azure Services

App Services can be seamlessly integrated with other Azure services like:

- **Azure SQL Database** for relational storage

- **Azure Storage** for blob, table, and queue storage

- **Azure Key Vault** for managing secrets

- **Azure Functions** for event-driven logic

- **Azure Logic Apps** for automating workflows

Example: Accessing secrets from Key Vault via App Service Managed Identity.

1. Enable System-assigned Managed Identity for your App Service.

2. Grant Get permissions on the secret in Key Vault.

3. In your application, use the Azure SDK to retrieve the secret:

```
const { DefaultAzureCredential } = require('@azure/identity');
const { SecretClient } = require('@azure/keyvault-secrets');
```

```
const credential = new DefaultAzureCredential();
const client = new
SecretClient("https://<YourVaultName>.vault.azure.net/",
credential);

async function getSecret() {
  const secret = await client.getSecret("DbPassword");
  console.log("Secret:", secret.value);
}
```

This promotes secure and centralized management of sensitive data.

Summary

Azure App Services provides a robust, flexible, and developer-friendly platform for building modern cloud applications. It simplifies deployment, enhances scalability, and integrates easily with other services in the Azure ecosystem. Whether you're building a small personal website or a large-scale enterprise-grade application, Azure App Services offers the tools and capabilities to accelerate development and streamline operations.

In the next section, we'll explore Azure Functions and how serverless architecture can complement or even replace traditional app hosting in specific scenarios.

Azure Functions and Serverless Architecture

Serverless computing has rapidly become one of the most transformative paradigms in modern cloud application development. It allows developers to focus solely on writing code without the need to manage infrastructure. Azure Functions, a key component of Microsoft Azure's serverless offering, enables developers to build event-driven applications with high scalability, low operational overhead, and flexible billing models based on actual execution time and resource consumption.

Understanding Serverless Architecture

In traditional application deployment, developers provision and manage servers to run their applications. Even with Platform-as-a-Service (PaaS) offerings like Azure App Services, developers still need to manage scaling, runtime environments, and sometimes even idle resources.

Serverless architecture abstracts these concerns entirely:

- **No server management:** You don't provision or manage servers.

- **Automatic scaling:** Functions scale automatically depending on the workload.

- **Micro-billing:** You only pay for the time your code is running.

Serverless is ideal for:

- Event-driven processes (e.g., HTTP triggers, timers, queue messages)

- Background jobs

- Real-time stream processing

- Lightweight APIs

- Prototypes and minimum viable products (MVPs)

Introduction to Azure Functions

Azure Functions is Azure's serverless compute service. You write small units of code called *functions*, which are triggered by specific events such as:

- HTTP requests

- Timer-based schedules

- Messages in a queue

- File uploads in a blob storage

- Events from Event Grid or Event Hub

Azure Functions supports various languages including:

- JavaScript / TypeScript (Node.js)

- C#

- Python

- Java

- PowerShell

- Custom handlers (e.g., Go, Rust)

Each function runs in a stateless environment and is isolated from others, allowing for easy scaling and modular application development.

Key Concepts and Terminology

- **Function App:** A container for one or more related functions. It provides shared resources like runtime version, app settings, and scaling configurations.

- **Triggers:** Define how a function is invoked. Each function has exactly one trigger.

- **Bindings:** Provide a declarative way to connect to other Azure services. Input bindings bring data into the function, while output bindings send data out.

- **Durable Functions:** An extension of Azure Functions that lets you write stateful workflows in a serverless environment.

Creating Your First Azure Function

You can create a function using the Azure Portal, Visual Studio, Visual Studio Code, or the Azure CLI. Here's an example using the CLI to create an HTTP-triggered function in JavaScript:

```
# Install Azure Functions Core Tools if not already installed
npm install -g azure-functions-core-tools@4 --unsafe-perm true

# Create a function app project
func init MyFunctionApp --javascript

# Navigate into the project
cd MyFunctionApp

# Create a new function with an HTTP trigger
func new --name HelloWorld --template "HTTP trigger"

# Run the function locally
func start
```

Once running, you'll see an HTTP endpoint like `http://localhost:7071/api/HelloWorld`. You can test it using a browser or curl:

```
curl http://localhost:7071/api/HelloWorld?name=Frahaan
```

Deploying to Azure

To deploy your function to Azure, first create a Function App in the cloud:

```
az group create --name MyResourceGroup --location eastus

az storage account create --name mystoragefuncapp --location eastus
--resource-group MyResourceGroup --sku Standard_LRS

az functionapp create --resource-group MyResourceGroup --
consumption-plan-location eastus --runtime node --functions-version
4 --name myuniquefunctionapp123 --storage-account mystoragefuncapp
```

Then publish your local function code to Azure:

```
func azure functionapp publish myuniquefunctionapp123
```

You'll receive a URL to access your function live on Azure.

Triggers and Bindings

HTTP Trigger

```
module.exports = async function (context, req) {
    const name = req.query.name || (req.body && req.body.name);
    context.res = {
        body: `Hello, ${name || "World"}!`
    };
};
```

Timer Trigger

```
module.exports = async function (context, myTimer) {
    var timeStamp = new Date().toISOString();
    context.log('Timer trigger function ran!', timeStamp);
};
```

```
function.json:

{
  "bindings": [
    {
      "name": "myTimer",
      "type": "timerTrigger",
      "direction": "in",
      "schedule": "0 */5 * * * *"
```

```
      }
   ]
}
```

This runs the function every 5 minutes.

Queue Trigger

```
module.exports = async function (context, myQueueItem) {
    context.log('Queue trigger function processed item',
myQueueItem);
};
```

```
function.json:

{
   "bindings": [
      {
         "name": "myQueueItem",
         "type": "queueTrigger",
         "direction": "in",
         "queueName": "myqueue-items",
         "connection": "AzureWebJobsStorage"
      }
   ]
}
```

Durable Functions

Durable Functions let you write stateful workflows using orchestrator functions, activity functions, and entities.

Orchestrator

```
const df = require("durable-functions");

module.exports = df.orchestrator(function* (context) {
    const outputs = [];

    outputs.push(yield context.df.callActivity("Hello", "Tokyo"));
    outputs.push(yield context.df.callActivity("Hello", "Seattle"));
    outputs.push(yield context.df.callActivity("Hello", "London"));
```

```
    return outputs;
});
```

Activity Function

```
module.exports = async function (context) {
    return `Hello ${context.bindings.name}!`;
};
```

Durable Functions are great for long-running workflows, chaining operations, or parallelizing function calls.

Scaling and Hosting Plans

Azure Functions offers different hosting options:

- **Consumption Plan (default):** You only pay for the time your functions run. Automatically scales based on demand.

- **Premium Plan:** Pre-warmed instances for predictable performance, VNET access, unlimited execution duration.

- **Dedicated (App Service) Plan:** Runs on dedicated VMs, useful if you need to run other services together or require specific scaling behavior.

Best Practices

1. **Keep Functions Small and Focused:** Each function should do one thing well and be independently testable.

2. **Use Durable Functions When Needed:** For stateful workflows or chaining logic.

3. **Externalize Configuration:** Use Azure App Configuration or environment variables for settings.

4. **Monitor with Application Insights:** Enables performance monitoring and failure tracking.

5. **Secure HTTP Triggers:** Use API keys or Azure Active Directory for authentication.

6. **Leverage Retry Policies:** Handle transient failures gracefully using built-in retry configurations.

Monitoring and Diagnostics

Azure Functions integrates natively with Application Insights. You can view:

- Invocation count

- Duration

- Failures

- Logs

- Traces

Enable it during Function App creation or link it later via the Azure Portal.

```
az functionapp update --name myuniquefunctionapp123 --resource-group
MyResourceGroup --set appInsightsKey=<your-key>
```

To log from code:

```
context.log('This is a log message');
context.log.error('Something went wrong');
```

You can also use custom metrics and telemetry.

Integration with Azure Services

Azure Functions easily connects with:

- **Blob Storage** for processing uploaded files

- **Event Grid** for reacting to cloud events

- **Cosmos DB** as a trigger or output

- **Service Bus** for messaging between services

- **SignalR** for real-time web apps

Example: Blob-triggered function

```
module.exports = async function (context, myBlob) {
    context.log(`Processed blob\n Name: ${context.bindingData.name}
\n Data: ${myBlob}`);
};
```

Binding configuration:

```json
{
  "bindings": [
    {
      "name": "myBlob",
      "type": "blobTrigger",
      "direction": "in",
      "path": "samples-workitems/{name}",
      "connection": "AzureWebJobsStorage"
    }
  ]
}
```

Summary

Azure Functions offers an elegant, flexible, and cost-effective approach to building applications that respond to events, scale automatically, and minimize infrastructure concerns. From simple HTTP APIs to complex, stateful orchestrations, Azure Functions enables developers to innovate rapidly and focus purely on code logic. The seamless integration with other Azure services, extensive language support, and development tooling make it a foundational component for modern cloud-native applications.

In the next section, we'll dive into Azure Virtual Machines to understand when and why to use Infrastructure-as-a-Service (IaaS) for workloads that require more control and customization.

Azure Virtual Machines

Azure Virtual Machines (VMs) provide Infrastructure-as-a-Service (IaaS) capabilities in the Microsoft Azure ecosystem. Unlike Platform-as-a-Service (PaaS) options like Azure App Services or serverless solutions such as Azure Functions, VMs offer full control over the operating system, installed software, and the environment. This makes them ideal for scenarios requiring custom configurations, legacy application support, or applications that cannot easily be containerized or run in abstracted environments.

What Are Azure Virtual Machines?

An Azure Virtual Machine is an on-demand, scalable computing resource hosted in the cloud. Each VM is a software emulation of a physical computer and includes:

- A virtual processor

- Memory

- Storage (OS disk, data disks, temporary disks)

- Network interface

- Operating system (Linux or Windows)

Users can choose from a variety of VM sizes, regions, images, and configurations based on their workload requirements.

Azure VMs are best suited for:

- Hosting legacy or traditional enterprise applications

- Running custom or niche software that requires full OS access

- Deploying infrastructure-heavy applications (e.g., databases, domain controllers)

- Creating development and test environments with complete control

- Running container hosts or orchestrators (e.g., Kubernetes with AKS)

Creating a Virtual Machine

You can create a VM using the Azure Portal, Azure CLI, PowerShell, or infrastructure-as-code tools like Bicep, ARM templates, or Terraform.

Here's a basic example using the Azure CLI to create a Linux VM:

```
# Create a resource group
az group create --name MyVMGroup --location eastus

# Create a virtual machine
az vm create \
  --resource-group MyVMGroup \
  --name MyUbuntuVM \
  --image UbuntuLTS \
  --admin-username azureuser \
  --generate-ssh-keys
```

This command:

- Creates a VM in the specified resource group

- Uses the Ubuntu LTS image

- Generates SSH keys if they don't already exist

- Configures a default virtual network and subnet

You can access the VM using SSH:

```
ssh azureuser@<public-ip>
```

Replace <public-ip> with the IP address outputted after VM creation.

Choosing the Right VM Size and Series

Azure offers a wide range of VM sizes categorized into different series:

- **B-series (Burstable):** Cost-effective for workloads that don't need full CPU all the time.

- **D-series:** Balanced CPU-to-memory ratio, general-purpose.

- **E-series:** Memory optimized for relational databases, in-memory analytics.

- **F-series:** Compute optimized for CPU-intensive applications.

- **M-series:** High memory VMs for SAP HANA, massive-scale databases.

- **N-series:** GPU-enabled for AI, ML, and visualization workloads.

- **H-series:** High performance computing (HPC).

Selecting the right VM depends on:

- CPU vs memory requirements

- Storage IOPS and throughput needs

- Network performance

- Workload type (web server, database, compute task, etc.)

You can resize VMs after deployment, though some changes may require restarting the VM.

Operating System and Image Options

Azure provides a wide variety of marketplace images, including:

- Windows Server (2016, 2019, 2022)

- Ubuntu, CentOS, Debian, Red Hat, SUSE

- Specialized images for SQL Server, Oracle, SAP, and more

- Custom images captured from existing VMs

You can also create your own custom image or use Azure Shared Image Gallery for managing and replicating images across regions.

Example for creating a Windows VM:

```
az vm create \
  --resource-group MyVMGroup \
  --name MyWinVM \
  --image Win2019Datacenter \
  --admin-username azureuser \
  --admin-password StrongPassword123!
```

VM Disks and Storage

Azure VMs have multiple types of disks:

- **OS Disk:** Contains the operating system. Managed by default.

- **Data Disks:** Optional disks for additional storage. Can be attached or detached.

- **Temporary Disk:** Local SSD used for page files or temporary data. Data is not persistent across reboots.

Managed disks come in various performance tiers:

- Standard HDD (cost-effective)

- Standard SSD (balanced)

- Premium SSD (high-performance)

- Ultra Disk (extremely high throughput and low latency)

To attach a new data disk:

```
az vm disk attach \
  --resource-group MyVMGroup \
  --vm-name MyUbuntuVM \
  --name MyDataDisk \
  --new \
  --size-gb 128
```

You must then partition and mount the disk on the VM.

Networking for VMs

Each Azure VM is connected to:

- **Virtual Network (VNet)**

- **Subnet**

- **Network Interface (NIC)**

- **Public and/or Private IP address**

You can define network security groups (NSGs) to restrict inbound/outbound traffic.

To open a port (e.g., for web server):

```
az vm open-port --port 80 --resource-group MyVMGroup --name MyUbuntuVM
```

Advanced scenarios might include:

- Load balancers for distributing traffic

- Application gateways with web application firewall (WAF)

- VPN gateways for hybrid cloud connectivity

- Azure Bastion for secure SSH/RDP without public IPs

Managing and Automating VMs

Azure provides several tools and services to manage and automate VM operations:

- **Azure Monitor:** Tracks performance metrics, usage, and diagnostics

- **Azure Automation:** Runbooks for scheduled tasks (e.g., start/stop VMs)

- **Update Management:** Apply OS patches and updates automatically

- **Azure Policy:** Enforce compliance rules (e.g., only specific VM sizes or regions)

For automation via Azure CLI:

```
# Stop a VM
az vm stop --resource-group MyVMGroup --name MyUbuntuVM

# Start a VM
az vm start --resource-group MyVMGroup --name MyUbuntuVM

# Delete a VM
az vm delete --resource-group MyVMGroup --name MyUbuntuVM --yes
```

Use tags to organize resources:

```
az resource tag --tags "environment=dev" --ids $(az vm show --name
MyUbuntuVM --resource-group MyVMGroup --query id -o tsv)
```

Security and Access Control

Security is critical when working with VMs:

- Use **Network Security Groups (NSGs)** to control traffic

- Use **Azure Bastion** to avoid exposing RDP/SSH directly

- **Enable Just-In-Time VM Access** to reduce attack surface

- Integrate with **Azure Defender** for threat detection

- Store sensitive credentials in **Azure Key Vault**

Role-Based Access Control (RBAC) allows you to restrict VM management capabilities:

```
az role assignment create \
  --assignee <userPrincipalName> \
  --role "Virtual Machine Contributor" \
```

```
  --scope $(az vm show --name MyUbuntuVM --resource-group MyVMGroup
--query id -o tsv)
```

This gives a user permission to manage the VM without full subscription access.

Backup and Disaster Recovery

Azure Backup can be used to protect your VMs against data loss:

```
# Enable backup
az backup protection enable-for-vm \
  --resource-group MyVMGroup \
  --vault-name MyRecoveryServicesVault \
  --vm MyUbuntuVM \
  --policy-name DefaultPolicy
```

For disaster recovery and regional failover, Azure Site Recovery replicates VMs to a secondary region. You can failover your workloads in case of an outage.

Cost Management

VM costs depend on:

- Size

- Region

- OS type (Linux VMs are generally cheaper than Windows)

- Disk and networking usage

- Licensing (Azure Hybrid Benefit allows bringing your own licenses)

Use cost-saving options:

- **Reserved Instances (1 or 3 years)**

- **Spot VMs** for non-critical, interruptible workloads

- **Auto-shutdown** for development or test VMs

You can configure auto-shutdown from the portal or via CLI:

```
az vm auto-shutdown --enabled true --resource-group MyVMGroup --name
MyUbuntuVM --time 1900
```

Monitoring and Diagnostics

Enable diagnostics during or after VM creation to collect performance counters, logs, and crash dumps.

Use Azure Monitor and Log Analytics to:

- View VM metrics (CPU, memory, disk)

- Configure alerts for unusual activity

- Analyze logs and visualize data

To enable diagnostics:

```
az vm diagnostics set \
  --resource-group MyVMGroup \
  --vm-name MyUbuntuVM \
  --settings ./diagnostics.json \
  --protected-settings ./protected-settings.json
```

Replace the JSON files with appropriate configurations.

Summary

Azure Virtual Machines provide the ultimate flexibility and control over your cloud infrastructure. They are powerful, versatile, and essential for certain workloads where abstraction and managed services fall short. With a wide variety of VM sizes, OS images, networking options, and integration with Azure's extensive service ecosystem, VMs can support nearly any computing scenario.

From development environments to full-scale production workloads, VMs are a core part of any Azure architect's toolkit. While they require more setup and maintenance than PaaS or serverless options, their power and flexibility make them indispensable in many real-world deployments.

In the next section, we'll explore Azure Storage and how to choose the right storage options for different types of application data.

Azure Storage Options: Blob, Table, Queue, and File Storage

Azure Storage is a foundational component of Microsoft Azure, providing durable, scalable, and secure storage solutions for a wide variety of use cases. Whether you're storing unstructured data like documents and images, working with structured NoSQL data, managing message queues for distributed systems, or mounting network file shares, Azure Storage has a service designed for your needs.

Azure Storage is built to handle massive-scale data with high availability, durability (via data replication), and integration with Azure's security and identity systems. In this section, we'll explore the core types of Azure Storage: Blob, Table, Queue, and File Storage, along with real-world use cases and configuration examples.

Core Concepts of Azure Storage

Before diving into the individual types, it's important to understand the general structure:

- **Storage Account**: A top-level namespace for accessing storage services. All types of data live under a storage account.

- **Containers / Tables / Queues / Shares**: Containers within the storage account for organizing data.

- **Blobs / Entities / Messages / Files**: The actual data.

Each storage account can include one or more of the following services:

- **Blob Storage**: For unstructured binary and text data.

- **Table Storage**: NoSQL key-value store.

- **Queue Storage**: Messaging store for asynchronous communication.

- **File Storage**: Managed file shares accessible via SMB protocol.

You interact with these services using Azure SDKs, REST APIs, Azure CLI, or Azure PowerShell.

Azure Blob Storage

Azure Blob Storage is designed for storing large volumes of unstructured data, such as images, videos, documents, and backups. It supports three types of blobs:

- **Block blobs**: Optimized for streaming and storing cloud objects.

- **Append blobs**: Ideal for append-only scenarios such as logging.

- **Page blobs**: Used for frequent read/write operations, often by virtual hard drives.

Blob Storage tiers:

- **Hot**: Frequently accessed data.

- **Cool**: Infrequently accessed data.

- **Archive**: Rarely accessed data, lowest cost, highest latency.

Creating Blob Storage

Using Azure CLI:

```
# Create a storage account
az storage account create \
  --name mystorageaccount123 \
  --resource-group MyResourceGroup \
  --location eastus \
  --sku Standard_LRS

# Create a blob container
az storage container create \
  --account-name mystorageaccount123 \
  --name mycontainer \
  --public-access off
```

Uploading and Downloading Blobs

```
# Upload a file
az storage blob upload \
  --account-name mystorageaccount123 \
  --container-name mycontainer \
  --name myimage.jpg \
  --file ./myimage.jpg

# Download a blob
az storage blob download \
  --account-name mystorageaccount123 \
  --container-name mycontainer \
  --name myimage.jpg \
  --file ./downloaded.jpg
```

Access and Security

- **Shared Access Signatures (SAS)** provide time-bound access.

- **Azure AD integration** for RBAC-based access control.

- **Private endpoints** for secure access via virtual networks.

Use Cases

- Media storage

- Application assets

- Backup and disaster recovery

- Data lake ingestion (with hierarchical namespace)

Azure Table Storage

Azure Table Storage is a NoSQL key-value store for rapid development and massive scalability. It stores structured, non-relational data in a schema-less design, making it ideal for scenarios where flexibility and speed are required over complex joins or relationships.

Structure

- **Table**: The container for rows.

- **Entity**: A row in the table.

- **Properties**: Columns of the entity.

- **PartitionKey + RowKey**: Composite key for uniquely identifying entities.

Creating a Table and Inserting Data

```
# Create a table
az storage table create \
  --name PeopleTable \
  --account-name mystorageaccount123

# Insert entity
az storage entity insert \
  --table-name PeopleTable \
```

```
  --account-name mystorageaccount123 \
  --entity PartitionKey=Employees RowKey=001 Name=Frahaan
Role=Developer
```

Querying Table Storage
```
az storage entity query \
  --account-name mystorageaccount123 \
  --table-name PeopleTable \
  --filter "PartitionKey eq 'Employees'"
```

Use Cases

- User metadata

- IoT telemetry

- Product catalogs

- Logging events

Note: For more advanced querying, consider **Azure Cosmos DB Table API**, which provides richer query features and global distribution.

Azure Queue Storage

Azure Queue Storage is a simple yet powerful service for storing messages that need to be processed asynchronously. It decouples components of cloud applications to improve scalability and reliability.

Each queue holds a list of messages (up to 64 KB each), and messages can be retained for up to seven days.

Creating a Queue
```
az storage queue create \
  --name myqueue \
  --account-name mystorageaccount123
```

Sending and Receiving Messages
```
# Send message
az storage message put \
  --account-name mystorageaccount123 \
```

```
  --queue-name myqueue \
  --content "Process order #123"

# Peek at messages (does not dequeue)
az storage message peek \
  --account-name mystorageaccount123 \
  --queue-name myqueue

# Receive and delete
az storage message get \
  --account-name mystorageaccount123 \
  --queue-name myqueue

az storage message delete \
  --account-name mystorageaccount123 \
  --queue-name myqueue \
  --id <message-id> \
  --pop-receipt <pop-receipt>
```

Integration

Queue Storage can integrate with:

- **Azure Functions** (Queue Trigger)

- **Event Grid**

- **Azure Logic Apps**

Use Cases

- Background job processing

- Workflow engines

- Notification queues

- Order processing systems

Azure File Storage

Azure Files offers shared storage for legacy applications or distributed systems. It provides a fully managed file share in the cloud using the Server Message Block (SMB) protocol and supports both Windows and Linux.

Creating a File Share

```
az storage share create \
  --name myshare \
  --account-name mystorageaccount123
```

Uploading and Downloading Files

```
# Upload
az storage file upload \
  --share-name myshare \
  --account-name mystorageaccount123 \
  --source ./localfile.txt

# Download
az storage file download \
  --share-name myshare \
  --account-name mystorageaccount123 \
  --path localfile.txt \
  --dest ./downloaded.txt
```

Mounting Azure Files

On a Windows machine:

```
net use Z: \\mystorageaccount123.file.core.windows.net\myshare
/u:mystorageaccount123 <storage-key>
```

On Linux:

```
sudo mount -t cifs
//mystorageaccount123.file.core.windows.net/myshare /mnt/azurefiles
-o vers=3.0,username=mystorageaccount123,password=<storage-
key>,dir_mode=0777,file_mode=0777,serverino
```

Use Cases

- File shares for VMs

- Configuration and install scripts

- Application logs

- Cross-platform sync environments

Performance, Redundancy, and Replication

Azure Storage supports several redundancy options:

- **LRS (Locally-redundant storage)**: Data is replicated within a single data center.

- **ZRS (Zone-redundant storage)**: Data is replicated across multiple zones within a region.

- **GRS (Geo-redundant storage)**: Data is replicated to a secondary region.

- **RA-GRS**: Same as GRS, but with read access to the secondary.

Select replication based on:

- SLA and compliance requirements

- Disaster recovery planning

- Cost considerations

Monitoring, Security, and Best Practices

Monitoring

Use **Azure Monitor** and **Storage Metrics** for:

- Capacity tracking

- Transaction and bandwidth usage

- Latency analysis

- Alerting and diagnostics

Security

- Use **Azure AD** and **RBAC** for secure access.

- Use **SAS tokens** for scoped, time-bound access.

- Enable **private endpoints** to restrict access over Azure VNet.

- Use **encryption at rest** (enabled by default) and **in-transit** with HTTPS.

Best Practices

1. **Choose the right service** for your workload type.

2. **Use tiers** (Hot, Cool, Archive) to manage cost-effectively.

3. **Partition data** in Table and Queue Storage using PartitionKey for performance.

4. **Rotate access keys** and monitor usage.

5. **Set lifecycle management policies** to automatically transition or delete blobs.

Example policy to move blobs to cool storage after 30 days:

```
{
  "rules": [
    {
      "name": "moveToCool",
      "enabled": true,
      "type": "Lifecycle",
      "definition": {
        "filters": {
          "blobTypes": ["blockBlob"]
        },
        "actions": {
          "baseBlob": {
            "tierToCool": {
              "daysAfterModificationGreaterThan": 30
            }
          }
        }
      }
    }
  ]
}
```

}

Summary

Azure Storage provides a flexible suite of services to store and manage all types of application data, from unstructured media files in Blob Storage to structured data in Table Storage, asynchronous workflows in Queue Storage, and shared drives via File Storage. Each service is designed to serve specific application needs while offering high availability, scalability, and tight security integration.

Selecting the right combination of these storage services can greatly simplify architecture, reduce costs, and improve performance. As your application grows, Azure Storage grows with it — providing a reliable foundation for any cloud-native or hybrid solution.

In the next chapter, we'll focus on how to manage these resources efficiently using tools like Azure Resource Manager, CLI, and PowerShell.

Chapter 4: Managing Azure Resources

Azure Resource Manager (ARM)

Azure Resource Manager (ARM) is the deployment and management framework for Azure resources. It enables you to provision, update, and delete resources in your Azure account through a unified interface. Whether you're working through the Azure Portal, CLI, PowerShell, SDKs, or REST APIs, ARM provides a consistent way to manage your infrastructure as code.

ARM plays a critical role in modern cloud operations, allowing developers and IT professionals to define infrastructure declaratively, automate deployments, enforce governance, and maintain a predictable environment through templates and resource group management.

Key Concepts of ARM

ARM introduces a few important abstractions that form the basis of how resources are managed in Azure:

- **Resource**: An individual item that is part of your solution (e.g., VM, storage account, web app).

- **Resource Group**: A container that holds related resources for an Azure solution. Resources can only belong to one resource group.

- **Resource Provider**: A service that provides a set of Azure resources. For example, Microsoft.Compute for VMs or Microsoft.Storage for storage accounts.

- **ARM Template**: A JSON (or Bicep) file that defines the infrastructure and configuration of your Azure solution.

Each operation performed in Azure goes through ARM, which validates, authenticates, and authorizes the request before executing it.

Benefits of ARM

- **Declarative Syntax**: Define your infrastructure using ARM templates or Bicep files.

- **Repeatable Deployments**: Easily replicate environments across multiple regions or stages.

- **Dependency Management**: Control the order of deployment and express dependencies between resources.

- **Integrated with RBAC**: Enforce fine-grained access control across resources and groups.

- **Tagging and Cost Tracking**: Use metadata to organize and monitor resources efficiently.

Working with ARM Templates

An ARM template is a JSON file that declaratively describes the desired state of your infrastructure. Here's an example of a basic ARM template that creates a storage account:

```json
{
  "$schema": "https://schema.management.azure.com/schemas/2019-04-01/deploymentTemplate.json#",
  "contentVersion": "1.0.0.0",
  "parameters": {
    "storageAccountName": {
      "type": "string"
    }
  },
  "resources": [
    {
      "type": "Microsoft.Storage/storageAccounts",
      "apiVersion": "2022-09-01",
      "name": "[parameters('storageAccountName')]",
      "location": "[resourceGroup().location]",
      "sku": {
        "name": "Standard_LRS"
      },
      "kind": "StorageV2",
      "properties": {}
    }
  ]
}
```

You can deploy this template using the Azure CLI:

```
az deployment group create \
```

```
  --resource-group MyResourceGroup \
  --template-file storage-account-template.json \
  --parameters storageAccountName=mystorageacct123
```

This will provision a new Storage Account with the specified name under the defined resource group.

Bicep: A Simpler Way to Use ARM

Bicep is a domain-specific language (DSL) that simplifies the authoring of ARM templates. It's more concise and readable than JSON and compiles down to a standard ARM template.

Here's the same storage account template written in Bicep:

```
param storageAccountName string

resource storageAccount 'Microsoft.Storage/storageAccounts@2022-09-01' = {
  name: storageAccountName
  location: resourceGroup().location
  sku: {
    name: 'Standard_LRS'
  }
  kind: 'StorageV2'
}
```

To deploy Bicep files:

```
az deployment group create \
  --resource-group MyResourceGroup \
  --template-file main.bicep \
  --parameters storageAccountName=mystorageacct123
```

Bicep dramatically reduces complexity and increases productivity, making it the preferred choice for infrastructure-as-code (IaC) in Azure.

Resource Group Management

Resource groups are essential for organizing, deploying, and managing Azure resources. They offer the following capabilities:

- Logical grouping for resources with shared lifecycle

- Simplified cost tracking and tagging

- Easier role-based access control (RBAC)

- One-click deletion of all resources in a group

Creating a Resource Group

```
az group create --name DevResourceGroup --location eastus
```

Viewing Resource Groups

```
az group list --output table
```

Deleting a Resource Group

```
az group delete --name DevResourceGroup --yes --no-wait
```

Deleting a resource group deletes all resources contained within it, making it a powerful tool for lifecycle management in dev/test scenarios.

Deployment Scopes and Modes

ARM supports deployments at different scopes:

- **Resource Group**

- **Subscription**

- **Management Group**

- **Tenant**

You can define the target scope within your template or through the CLI.

Deployment modes:

- **Incremental**: Adds resources or updates existing ones, leaving the rest unchanged.

- **Complete**: Removes resources not defined in the template.

Use complete mode with caution:

```
az deployment group create \
  --resource-group DevGroup \
  --template-file main.json \
  --mode Complete
```

Linked and Nested Templates

For complex environments, break templates into multiple files:

- **Linked templates** reference external templates.

- **Nested templates** embed other templates within the main file.

This modular approach improves maintainability and reuse.

Example:

```
{
  "type": "Microsoft.Resources/deployments",
  "apiVersion": "2022-09-01",
  "name": "nestedDeployment",
  "properties": {
    "mode": "Incremental",
    "templateLink": {
      "uri": "https://mycdn.com/templates/storage.json",
      "contentVersion": "1.0.0.0"
    },
    "parameters": {
      "storageAccountName": {
        "value": "mylinkedstorage"
      }
    }
  }
}
```

Deployment Scripts and Outputs

You can include scripts in templates for post-deployment configuration using `Microsoft.Resources/deploymentScripts`.

ARM also supports output values to pass results from one template to another:

```
"outputs": {
  "storageUri": {
    "type": "string",
    "value":
"[reference(resourceId('Microsoft.Storage/storageAccounts',
parameters('storageAccountName'))).primaryEndpoints.blob]"
  }
}
```

Use these outputs in CI/CD workflows or chaining deployments together.

Tags and Policies with ARM

Tags are key-value pairs applied to resources and groups to organize and filter your infrastructure:

```
az resource tag \
  --tags environment=production owner=frahaan \
  --ids $(az storage account show --name mystorageacct123 --
resource-group DevResourceGroup --query id -o tsv)
```

Policies enforce governance:

- Limit resource types or locations

- Enforce naming conventions

- Require specific tags

Assign a policy with ARM:

```
az policy assignment create \
  --name enforceTag \
  --policy definition.json \
```

```
  --scope /subscriptions/{subscription-
id}/resourceGroups/DevResourceGroup
```

Integrating ARM with CI/CD

ARM templates and Bicep files integrate seamlessly into DevOps pipelines:

Azure DevOps YAML Task

```
- task: AzureResourceManagerTemplateDeployment@3
  inputs:
    deploymentScope: 'Resource Group'
    azureResourceManagerConnection: 'AzureServiceConnection'
    subscriptionId: 'xxxx-xxxx-xxxx-xxxx'
    action: 'Create Or Update Resource Group'
    resourceGroupName: 'DevResourceGroup'
    location: 'East US'
    templateLocation: 'Linked artifact'
    csmFile: 'infrastructure/main.bicep'
    deploymentMode: 'Incremental'
```

GitHub Actions

```
- name: Deploy ARM Template
  uses: azure/arm-deploy@v1
  with:
    scope: resourcegroup
    resourceGroupName: DevResourceGroup
    template: ./main.bicep
    parameters: storageAccountName=mystorageacct123
```

These automations allow you to treat infrastructure the same way as application code, enabling faster iterations, consistency, and traceability.

Summary

Azure Resource Manager (ARM) is the backbone of Azure resource provisioning and governance. By leveraging ARM templates or Bicep, you can manage your infrastructure declaratively, enforce security and compliance policies, automate deployment pipelines, and organize resources with precision.

Whether you're provisioning a single storage account or an entire enterprise-grade architecture, ARM equips you with the tools and practices to achieve predictable, scalable, and manageable cloud infrastructure.

In the following section, we'll focus on creating and managing Resource Groups, the building blocks for organizing Azure deployments.

Creating and Managing Resource Groups

In Azure, resource groups are the logical containers that hold related resources such as virtual machines, storage accounts, web apps, databases, and virtual networks. They provide a unified way to deploy, manage, and monitor resources as a single unit based on lifecycle, permissions, and tags. Understanding how to effectively create and manage resource groups is essential for organizing resources, applying governance, and simplifying operations across your cloud infrastructure.

What is a Resource Group?

A resource group in Azure is a container that holds related resources for an application or workload. All resources in a resource group share the same lifecycle and can be deployed, updated, and deleted together.

Key Characteristics:

- A resource can belong to only one resource group.

- A resource group can contain resources from multiple regions.

- Resource groups allow for consolidated billing and tagging.

- Access control policies can be applied at the resource group level using RBAC.

Resource groups play a foundational role in infrastructure organization and are integral to both manual and automated deployment strategies.

Creating Resource Groups

You can create resource groups using multiple methods: Azure Portal, Azure CLI, PowerShell, ARM templates, Bicep, and SDKs. The most common approach is through the Azure CLI or Portal.

Using Azure CLI

```
az group create --name DevResourceGroup --location eastus
```

This command creates a resource group named `DevResourceGroup` in the `East US` region.

Using PowerShell

```
New-AzResourceGroup -Name DevResourceGroup -Location "East US"
```

Using Azure Portal

1. Navigate to **Resource groups** in the Azure Portal.

2. Click **+ Create**.

3. Provide a **Resource Group Name** and select a **Region**.

4. Click **Review + Create**, then **Create**.

Using Bicep

```
targetScope = 'subscription'

resource devGroup 'Microsoft.Resources/resourceGroups@2021-04-01' = {
  name: 'DevResourceGroup'
  location: 'eastus'
}
```

Deploy with:

```
az deployment sub create --location eastus --template-file main.bicep
```

Viewing and Listing Resource Groups

To list all resource groups in your subscription:

```
az group list --output table
```

To get details of a specific resource group:

```
az group show --name DevResourceGroup
```

PowerShell equivalent:

```
Get-AzResourceGroup -Name DevResourceGroup
```

Updating and Tagging Resource Groups

Tags allow you to associate metadata with your resource groups, which is useful for billing, automation, and management.

```
az group update --name DevResourceGroup --tags
Environment=Development Owner=Frahaan
```

You can also remove or modify tags later:

```
az group update --name DevResourceGroup --set tags.Owner=NewOwner
az group update --name DevResourceGroup --remove tags.Environment
```

PowerShell equivalent:

```
Set-AzResourceGroup -Name DevResourceGroup -Tag
@{Environment="Development"; Owner="Frahaan"}
```

Moving Resources Between Resource Groups

Azure allows you to move most types of resources between resource groups or even between subscriptions, with certain limitations.

```
az resource move \
  --destination-group NewResourceGroup \
  --ids $(az resource show --name myVM --resource-group
DevResourceGroup --resource-type Microsoft.Compute/virtualMachines -
-query id -o tsv)
```

Ensure that:

- The destination resource group is in the same region if the resource type doesn't support cross-region moves.

- Some services (e.g., App Service with certain configurations) may not support moving.

To move via Portal:

1. Select the resources to move.

2. Click **Move** > **Move to another resource group**.

3. Choose the target group and validate.

Deleting Resource Groups

When a resource group is deleted, all resources within it are also deleted. This makes deletion a powerful but potentially dangerous operation.

Azure CLI

```
az group delete --name DevResourceGroup --yes --no-wait
```

PowerShell

```
Remove-AzResourceGroup -Name DevResourceGroup -Force
```

This command deletes the group and all its associated resources. Always double-check before running this command in production environments.

Organizing Resource Groups Effectively

The way you organize your resource groups depends on your organization's structure, environment, and operational practices.

Common Organizational Models:

1. **By Application**: Group all resources for a specific application together.

2. **By Environment**: Separate resource groups for dev, test, staging, and production.

3. **By Department or Team**: Helps with access control and cost tracking.

4. **By Lifecycle**: Temporary vs permanent infrastructure.

Recommendations:

- Avoid mixing unrelated resources in the same group.

- Use consistent naming conventions (`[env]-[app]-[component]`).

- Apply governance using Azure Policy and management groups.

Example naming:

- `prod-web-frontend-rg`

- `dev-data-ingestion-rg`

- `shared-networking-rg`

Role-Based Access Control (RBAC)

You can assign roles at the resource group level to control who can manage the resources inside.

```
az role assignment create \
  --assignee user@example.com \
  --role "Contributor" \
  --scope /subscriptions/<sub-id>/resourceGroups/DevResourceGroup
```

This limits the user to managing only the resources inside the specified group. This is useful for delegating control to development teams or external vendors.

Common roles:

- **Reader** – View-only access.

- **Contributor** – Full management access without RBAC permission changes.

- **Owner** – Full access including access control changes.

Resource Group Deployment with Templates

You can target a resource group when deploying infrastructure as code.

```
az deployment group create \
  --resource-group DevResourceGroup \
  --template-file main.bicep
```

This is the most common deployment target when using ARM or Bicep templates.

Outputs from the template can also be used across deployment stages or returned to CI/CD pipelines.

Monitoring and Auditing Resource Groups

Use **Azure Monitor** and **Activity Logs** to track changes and monitor performance.

To view recent changes:

```
az monitor activity-log list --resource-group DevResourceGroup --
max-events 10 --output table
```

This helps you identify who modified a resource, what actions were taken, and whether any failures occurred.

Integrate with **Azure Policy** to enforce tagging, region restrictions, and naming conventions:

```
az policy assignment create \
  --policy definition.json \
  --scope /subscriptions/<sub-id>/resourceGroups/DevResourceGroup \
  --name requireTagEnvironment
```

Locking Resource Groups

Resource locks prevent accidental deletion or modification.

```
az lock create \
  --name "ProtectRG" \
  --lock-type CanNotDelete \
  --resource-group DevResourceGroup
```

Lock types:

- **CanNotDelete**: Resources can be read and modified, but not deleted.

- **ReadOnly**: Resources can only be read; no modifications or deletions.

Remove a lock:

```
az lock delete --name "ProtectRG" --resource-group DevResourceGroup
```

Locks are especially important for production and critical infrastructure.

Summary

Resource groups are a vital building block in Azure for organizing and managing your cloud assets. By grouping resources based on application, environment, or team, you simplify operations, improve access control, and optimize cost management. Azure provides rich tooling—CLI, Portal, PowerShell, and Bicep—for creating, tagging, securing, and monitoring resource groups effectively.

With a solid resource group strategy in place, you're well-equipped to build scalable, maintainable, and well-governed cloud environments. In the next section, we'll dive deeper into Azure's Role-Based Access Control (RBAC) and how it enables fine-grained permissions across your resource hierarchy.

Understanding Role-Based Access Control (RBAC)

Role-Based Access Control (RBAC) is a fundamental security and governance feature in Microsoft Azure that allows administrators to manage who has access to Azure resources, what they can do with those resources, and what areas they have access to. RBAC plays a critical role in ensuring the principle of least privilege, which helps secure your environment, reduce human error, and maintain regulatory compliance.

By defining roles and assigning them to users, groups, or applications, you can tailor access permissions to match your organizational structure and operational requirements.

RBAC Key Concepts

To fully utilize RBAC, it's essential to understand its core components:

- **Security Principal**: The user, group, service principal (application), or managed identity that requests access.

- **Role Definition**: A collection of permissions that can be assigned to security principals. Each role defines allowed actions (read, write, delete, etc.) on Azure resources.

- **Scope**: The level at which access applies. Scopes can be assigned at four levels:

    - **Management Group**

    - **Subscription**

    - **Resource Group**

    - **Resource**

- **Role Assignment**: The link between a security principal, role definition, and scope. This assignment determines what the principal can do.

RBAC evaluates a user's access based on the combination of these three elements.

Built-In Roles

Azure provides more than 70 built-in roles to cover common access scenarios. Some commonly used ones include:

- **Owner**: Full access to all resources, including assigning RBAC roles.

- **Contributor**: Can manage all resources but cannot assign roles.

- **Reader**: Can view everything but cannot make changes.

- **User Access Administrator**: Can manage RBAC assignments but not resources.

- **Virtual Machine Contributor**: Can manage VMs but not the network or storage resources.

You can view all built-in roles using:

```
az role definition list --output table
```

Or for a specific role:

```
az role definition show --name Contributor
```

Assigning Roles

To assign a role, you specify:

- The **security principal** (user, group, app)

- The **role**

- The **scope**

Assigning a role using Azure CLI:

```
az role assignment create \
  --assignee user@example.com \
  --role Contributor \
  --scope /subscriptions/<subscription-
id>/resourceGroups/MyResourceGroup
```

This gives the user Contributor permissions over the MyResourceGroup.

Assigning at different scopes:

- At **subscription** level:

```
az role assignment create \
  --assignee user@example.com \
  --role Reader \
  --scope /subscriptions/<subscription-id>
```

- At **resource** level:

```
az role assignment create \
  --assignee user@example.com \
  --role "Virtual Machine Contributor" \
  --scope /subscriptions/<sub-
id>/resourceGroups/RG1/providers/Microsoft.Compute/virtualMachines/m
yVM
```

You can also assign roles using the Azure Portal:

1. Go to the resource/resource group/subscription.

2. Select **Access control (IAM)**.

3. Click **+ Add > Add role assignment**.

4. Choose role, assignee, and scope.

Viewing and Removing Role Assignments

To view role assignments:

```
az role assignment list --assignee user@example.com --output table
```

To remove an assignment:

```
az role assignment delete \
  --assignee user@example.com \
  --role Contributor \
  --scope /subscriptions/<subscription-
id>/resourceGroups/MyResourceGroup
```

Custom Roles

Built-in roles may not always meet specific business requirements. Custom roles allow you to define permissions more precisely.

A custom role is defined in JSON and includes:

- Name

- Description

- Actions

- NotActions

- DataActions (for data plane)

- NotDataActions

- AssignableScopes

Example Custom Role

```
{
  "Name": "Custom Storage Reader",
  "IsCustom": true,
  "Description": "Read-only access to storage accounts",
  "Actions": [
    "Microsoft.Storage/storageAccounts/read",
    "Microsoft.Storage/storageAccounts/listkeys/action"
  ],
  "NotActions": [],
  "AssignableScopes": ["/subscriptions/<subscription-id>"]
}
```

Create the custom role:

```
az role definition create --role-definition custom-role.json
```

Assign it just like a built-in role.

RBAC vs. Azure AD Roles

It's important to differentiate Azure RBAC roles from Azure Active Directory roles:

- **Azure RBAC**: Controls access to Azure resources (compute, storage, networking).

- **Azure AD Roles**: Controls directory-wide functions (e.g., user management, group creation).

For example, a **Global Administrator** (Azure AD role) can manage tenant-wide settings, while a **Contributor** (Azure RBAC) can manage services within a specific resource group.

You may need to assign roles across both systems for full functionality. For instance, an app may require:

- RBAC to access a storage account

- Azure AD App permissions to read user profiles

Using RBAC with Managed Identities

Managed Identities (system-assigned or user-assigned) allow Azure resources to authenticate securely to services without managing credentials.

To grant access using RBAC:

```
az role assignment create \
  --assignee <principal-id-of-identity> \
  --role Reader \
  --scope /subscriptions/<sub-id>/resourceGroups/MyResourceGroup
```

This is essential for automating deployments, securing apps, or integrating services like Azure Functions with Key Vault.

Auditing and Monitoring RBAC

Activity Logs and Azure Monitor provide insights into RBAC operations:

- Track who made a role assignment or deletion.

- Detect privilege escalations.

- Audit changes for compliance.

To list RBAC-related activity logs:

```
az monitor activity-log list \
  --resource-group MyResourceGroup \
  --max-events 20 \
  --query
"[?operationName.value=='Microsoft.Authorization/roleAssignments/wri
te']"
```

Integrate with Log Analytics for alerting and long-term retention.

RBAC Best Practices

1. **Follow Least Privilege**: Assign only the permissions required.

2. **Use Resource Groups**: Apply scoped roles at the group level to isolate apps or teams.

3. **Limit Owner Role Usage**: Use sparingly and only for highly trusted individuals.

4. **Review Assignments Regularly**: Audit who has what access and why.

5. **Use Groups, Not Individuals**: Assign roles to AD groups for easier management.

6. **Automate Role Assignments**: Use IaC tools (e.g., Bicep, ARM) for consistency.

Example Bicep snippet to assign a role:

```
resource roleAssignment
'Microsoft.Authorization/roleAssignments@2020-10-01-preview' = {
  name: guid(subscription().id, 'Reader', principalId)
  properties: {
    roleDefinitionId:
subscriptionResourceId('Microsoft.Authorization/roleDefinitions',
'acdd72a7-3385-48ef-bd42-f606fba81ae7')
    principalId: principalId
    principalType: 'User'
  }
}
```

Replace `principalId` with the object ID of the user or group.

Summary

Role-Based Access Control (RBAC) is an essential component of any secure and scalable Azure architecture. It empowers you to manage access with fine-grained precision, ensuring users, services, and applications have the right permissions at the right scopes. Whether you're assigning built-in roles, designing custom policies, or integrating with managed identities, RBAC gives you the tools to enforce security without sacrificing agility.

As your Azure environment grows in complexity, implementing a sound RBAC strategy is key to operational success, governance, and regulatory compliance. In the next section, we will explore how to use Azure CLI and PowerShell to automate and streamline Azure resource management.

Using Azure CLI and PowerShell

The Azure Command-Line Interface (Azure CLI) and Azure PowerShell are powerful tools for managing Azure resources programmatically. They allow developers, system administrators, and DevOps professionals to automate tasks, manage infrastructure at scale, and streamline operations. Understanding how to use these tools effectively can greatly enhance productivity and reduce the risk of manual errors in cloud environments.

Both tools can perform most of the same tasks but cater to different audiences. Azure CLI is optimized for cross-platform scripting and Bash-style commands, while Azure PowerShell is best suited for users familiar with the PowerShell environment, particularly Windows administrators.

Azure CLI vs. Azure PowerShell: A Comparison

Feature	Azure CLI	Azure PowerShell
Language	Command-line (Bash-style)	PowerShell scripting
Platform	Cross-platform	Cross-platform
Syntax Style	Simple and compact	Verb-Noun (e.g., `Get-AzVM`)
Best For	Developers, Linux/macOS users	Sysadmins, Windows users
Output Formats	JSON, Table, TSV	Object-oriented (PSObjects)

In practice, many Azure professionals use both depending on the scenario.

Installing Azure CLI and PowerShell

Azure CLI

Install the Azure CLI on macOS, Linux, or Windows:

```
# On Windows (PowerShell)
Invoke-WebRequest -Uri https://aka.ms/installazurecliwindows -OutFile .\AzureCLI.msi; Start-Process .\AzureCLI.msi

# On macOS
brew install azure-cli

# On Ubuntu
curl -sL https://aka.ms/InstallAzureCLIDeb | sudo bash
```

Verify installation:

```
az --version
```

Azure PowerShell

Install the Az module using PowerShell:

```
Install-Module -Name Az -Scope CurrentUser -Repository PSGallery -Force
```

Verify installation:

```
Get-Module -Name Az -ListAvailable
```

You may need to import the module if not already loaded:

```
Import-Module Az
```

Logging In and Setting Context

Azure CLI

```
az login
az account set --subscription "<subscription-id-or-name>"
```

Azure PowerShell

```
Connect-AzAccount
Set-AzContext -SubscriptionId "<subscription-id>"
```

You can use az account list or Get-AzSubscription to see available subscriptions.

Managing Resource Groups

Azure CLI

```
az group create --name DevGroup --location eastus
az group list --output table
az group delete --name DevGroup --yes --no-wait
```

PowerShell

```powershell
New-AzResourceGroup -Name DevGroup -Location "East US"
Get-AzResourceGroup
Remove-AzResourceGroup -Name DevGroup -Force
```

Managing Virtual Machines

Create a VM (Azure CLI)

```
az vm create \
  --resource-group DevGroup \
  --name MyVM \
  --image UbuntuLTS \
  --admin-username azureuser \
  --generate-ssh-keys
```

Create a VM (PowerShell)

```powershell
$cred = Get-Credential
New-AzVM -ResourceGroupName "DevGroup" -Name "MyVM" -Location "East
US" -VirtualNetworkName "MyVNet" -SubnetName "MySubnet" -
SecurityGroupName "MyNSG" -PublicIpAddressName "MyIP" -Credential
$cred -ImageName "UbuntuLTS"
```

Managing Storage Accounts

Azure CLI

```
az storage account create \
  --name mystorageacct \
  --resource-group DevGroup \
  --location eastus \
  --sku Standard_LRS
```

PowerShell

```powershell
New-AzStorageAccount -ResourceGroupName "DevGroup" -Name
"mystorageacct" -Location "East US" -SkuName "Standard_LRS" -Kind
"StorageV2"
```

Working with ARM Templates

You can deploy ARM templates or Bicep files via both tools.

Azure CLI

```
az deployment group create \
  --resource-group DevGroup \
  --template-file main.bicep \
  --parameters storageAccountName=mystorageacct123
```

PowerShell

```
New-AzResourceGroupDeployment -ResourceGroupName "DevGroup" -
TemplateFile "./main.bicep" -storageAccountName "mystorageacct123"
```

Both tools support parameter files and inline parameters.

Managing Role Assignments

Azure CLI

```
az role assignment create \
  --assignee user@example.com \
  --role Contributor \
  --scope /subscriptions/<subscription-id>/resourceGroups/DevGroup
```

PowerShell

```
New-AzRoleAssignment -ObjectId "<user-object-id>" -
RoleDefinitionName "Contributor" -Scope
"/subscriptions/<subscription-id>/resourceGroups/DevGroup"
```

You can list assignments using az role assignment list or Get-
AzRoleAssignment.

Monitoring and Diagnostics

Azure CLI

```
az monitor activity-log list --max-events 10 --output table
```

PowerShell

```
Get-AzActivityLog -MaxRecord 10
```

To enable diagnostics on a VM:

```
az vm diagnostics set \
  --resource-group DevGroup \
  --vm-name MyVM \
  --settings ./diagnostics.json \
  --protected-settings ./protected-settings.json
```

Using Scripts and Automation

Both Azure CLI and PowerShell are ideal for writing scripts. Example Bash script:

```bash
#!/bin/bash
az login
az group create --name DevOpsGroup --location eastus
az storage account create --name mystorageacct --resource-group
DevOpsGroup --location eastus --sku Standard_LRS
```

Example PowerShell script:

```
Connect-AzAccount
New-AzResourceGroup -Name DevOpsGroup -Location "East US"
New-AzStorageAccount -ResourceGroupName "DevOpsGroup" -Name
"mystorageacct" -Location "East US" -SkuName "Standard_LRS" -Kind
"StorageV2"
```

These scripts can be integrated into CI/CD pipelines, task schedulers, or executed as part of larger infrastructure orchestration workflows.

Troubleshooting and Tips

- Use `--debug` or `--verbose` in Azure CLI for detailed logs.

- Pipe output to `jq` (CLI) or use `Select-Object`/`Where-Object` in PowerShell for filtering.

- Use `az find` to discover commands:

```
az find "vm create"
```

- Use `Get-Help` in PowerShell:

```
Get-Help New-AzVM -Detailed
```

- Set default values:

```
az configure --defaults group=DevGroup location=eastus
```

This reduces the need to specify common parameters repeatedly.

Summary

Azure CLI and PowerShell are essential tools in any cloud engineer's toolkit. Whether you're managing resources interactively or automating large-scale deployments, these tools offer the control, flexibility, and consistency required for modern cloud operations.

While Azure CLI excels with concise commands and scripting in Unix-like environments, PowerShell is unmatched in its ability to work with rich objects and integrate into enterprise Windows workflows. Mastering both provides a significant advantage when building and managing Azure infrastructure.

In the next chapter, we'll begin developing applications on Azure, starting with deploying web applications and integrating them with modern CI/CD pipelines.

Chapter 5: Developing Applications on Azure

Deploying Web Applications

In the modern application lifecycle, the ability to deploy web applications rapidly, reliably, and securely is fundamental. Azure offers a robust platform for hosting and deploying web apps, with powerful tools and services that make the process efficient, scalable, and integrated with a wide range of development tools. This section will walk you through everything you need to know to deploy web applications on Microsoft Azure, including setting up environments, choosing the right service, and automating deployments.

Choosing the Right Azure Web Hosting Service

Before deploying a web application, it's essential to determine the appropriate Azure hosting service based on the application's needs:

- **Azure App Service**: Ideal for most web applications. Supports multiple programming languages and frameworks including .NET, .NET Core, Java, Ruby, Node.js, PHP, and Python.

- **Azure Static Web Apps**: Best for static front-end apps with serverless backends using Azure Functions.

- **Azure Kubernetes Service (AKS)**: For containerized apps needing orchestration.

- **Azure Virtual Machines**: Suitable for legacy applications or custom server setups.

For most beginner to intermediate use cases, **Azure App Service** provides the optimal balance between ease of use, scalability, and flexibility.

Creating an Azure App Service Web App

To deploy a web app, you first need to create a Web App resource on Azure. This can be done using the Azure Portal, Azure CLI, or ARM templates.

Using Azure CLI:

```
# Log in to Azure
az login

# Set your preferred subscription
az account set --subscription "Your Subscription Name"
```

```
# Create a Resource Group
az group create --name MyResourceGroup --location "East US"

# Create an App Service Plan
az appservice plan create --name MyAppServicePlan --resource-group
MyResourceGroup --sku B1 --is-linux

# Create a Web App
az webapp create --resource-group MyResourceGroup --plan
MyAppServicePlan --name MyUniqueAppName --runtime "NODE|18-lts"
```

Deploying Your Code

Once the Web App is created, you can deploy your application using various methods:

1. Using GitHub Actions for CI/CD

Azure App Service can be connected to a GitHub repository to set up continuous deployment.

Steps:

1. Go to your Web App in the Azure Portal.

2. Navigate to **Deployment Center**.

3. Select **GitHub**, authorize the connection, and choose the repository and branch.

4. Azure will automatically configure GitHub Actions for your app.

The GitHub Actions workflow might look like this for a Node.js app:

```
name: Deploy Node.js app to Azure Web App

on:
  push:
    branches:
      - main

jobs:
  build-and-deploy:
    runs-on: ubuntu-latest
    steps:
```

```
- name: Checkout code
  uses: actions/checkout@v2

- name: Set up Node.js
  uses: actions/setup-node@v2
  with:
    node-version: '18'

- name: Install dependencies
  run: npm install

- name: Build the app
  run: npm run build

- name: Deploy to Azure Web App
  uses: azure/webapps-deploy@v2
  with:
    app-name: 'MyUniqueAppName'
    publish-profile: ${{
secrets.AZUREAPPSERVICE_PUBLISHPROFILE }}
    package: .
```

To generate the `AZUREAPPSERVICE_PUBLISHPROFILE` secret:

- In the Azure Portal, go to your Web App.

- Click **Get Publish Profile** and copy the XML content.

- In GitHub, go to your repository settings → Secrets → Actions → New repository secret, and paste the profile.

2. Using Azure CLI for Manual Deployment

For simpler scenarios or development testing, you can use Azure CLI to deploy your app directly from a local machine.

```
az webapp deployment source config-zip \
  --resource-group MyResourceGroup \
  --name MyUniqueAppName \
  --src myapp.zip
```

Make sure `myapp.zip` contains your application files with the correct structure.

Environment Configuration

Azure allows you to configure environment variables (Application Settings) easily via the Azure Portal or CLI.

```
az webapp config appsettings set \
  --name MyUniqueAppName \
  --resource-group MyResourceGroup \
  --settings NODE_ENV=production API_URL=https://api.example.com
```

These settings will be available in your app as environment variables, e.g., `process.env.NODE_ENV`.

Custom Domains and SSL

To make your web app production-ready, you'll want to map a custom domain and enable SSL.

1. Go to your Web App in the Azure Portal.

2. Navigate to **Custom domains**.

3. Add your domain name and verify ownership via TXT or A record.

4. Once verified, bind the domain.

5. Navigate to **TLS/SSL settings** and enable HTTPS.

Azure also supports free App Service-managed certificates.

Scaling Your Web App

Azure App Services support both vertical and horizontal scaling.

- **Vertical Scaling**: Upgrading the App Service Plan to a more powerful instance (e.g., from B1 to S1).

- **Horizontal Scaling**: Increasing the number of instances to handle more traffic.

```
az appservice plan update \
  --name MyAppServicePlan \
  --resource-group MyResourceGroup \
```

```
--number-of-workers 3
```

Monitoring and Diagnostics

Use Azure Monitor and Application Insights to get insights into your application's performance.

To enable Application Insights:

1. Go to your Web App in Azure Portal.

2. Under **Settings**, click **Application Insights**.

3. Enable it and choose/create an Application Insights resource.

This will allow you to track request rates, response times, exceptions, and even user behavior.

Troubleshooting Common Issues

App Doesn't Start or Crashes

- Check logs under **Log stream** or enable **Application Logging**.

- Validate environment variables.

- Review the runtime stack and version.

Deployment Fails

- Ensure the ZIP or GitHub Action contains the correct structure.

- Check quota limits on your App Service Plan.

Permissions Issues

- Validate that the deployment credentials or GitHub secrets are correctly configured.

Summary

Deploying web applications to Azure is a streamlined process, whether you choose manual deployments or automated CI/CD pipelines. Azure App Service provides an enterprise-grade hosting platform with powerful integrations, scaling options, and monitoring capabilities. By leveraging tools like the Azure CLI, GitHub Actions, and the Azure Portal, developers can focus more on building their applications rather than managing infrastructure.

Configuring Continuous Integration/Continuous Deployment (CI/CD)

Continuous Integration and Continuous Deployment (CI/CD) are crucial practices in modern application development that ensure code changes are tested, integrated, and deployed quickly and reliably. Microsoft Azure provides a suite of tools and services that allow developers to configure and automate the CI/CD process seamlessly, with support for GitHub Actions, Azure DevOps Pipelines, Bitbucket, GitLab, Jenkins, and other third-party services.

This section will guide you through configuring CI/CD pipelines using two of the most popular methods on Azure: **Azure DevOps Pipelines** and **GitHub Actions**. We'll cover setting up the pipeline, automating builds and tests, deploying to Azure App Service, and managing secrets and environments effectively.

Understanding CI/CD on Azure

- **Continuous Integration (CI)** is the practice of automatically building and testing code every time a change is pushed to a version control repository.

- **Continuous Deployment (CD)** takes CI a step further by automatically deploying the build to a staging or production environment after successful tests.

CI/CD significantly reduces integration issues, provides quicker feedback, and enables faster iterations.

Prerequisites

To follow along, you will need:

- An active Azure subscription

- A deployed Azure App Service (Web App)

- A code repository hosted on GitHub or Azure Repos

- Basic familiarity with Git

CI/CD with Azure DevOps Pipelines

Azure DevOps offers powerful and flexible CI/CD pipelines tightly integrated with Azure resources.

Step 1: Create a Project in Azure DevOps

1. Go to https://dev.azure.com/ and sign in.

2. Click "New Project".

3. Enter a project name and choose visibility.

4. Click "Create".

Step 2: Set Up a Repository or Connect to GitHub

- You can use Azure Repos or connect to an external Git repository like GitHub or Bitbucket.

- For GitHub, choose **Service connections** from Project settings and link your GitHub account.

Step 3: Create a Build Pipeline

1. Navigate to **Pipelines > Pipelines**, then click **New Pipeline**.

2. Choose your repository.

3. Select **YAML** configuration.

4. Azure will scan and suggest templates. Choose the one that matches your stack.

For a Node.js project, a typical `azure-pipelines.yml` might look like this:

```
trigger:
  branches:
    include:
      - main

pool:
  vmImage: 'ubuntu-latest'

steps:
- task: NodeTool@0
  inputs:
```

```
    versionSpec: '18.x'
  displayName: 'Install Node.js'

- script: |
    npm install
    npm run build
  displayName: 'Install and Build'

- task: ArchiveFiles@2
  inputs:
    rootFolderOrFile: '$(System.DefaultWorkingDirectory)'
    includeRootFolder: false
    archiveType: zip
    archiveFile: '$(Build.ArtifactStagingDirectory)/app.zip'
    replaceExistingArchive: true

- task: PublishBuildArtifacts@1
  inputs:
    PathtoPublish: '$(Build.ArtifactStagingDirectory)'
    ArtifactName: 'drop'
```

Step 4: Release Pipeline for Deployment

1. Go to **Pipelines > Releases** and click **New pipeline**.

2. Add an artifact and link it to the build output.

3. Add a stage and choose **Azure App Service Deployment**.

4. Configure the connection to your Azure Web App.

5. Enable continuous deployment trigger.

You can add approvals, conditions, and additional environments such as staging or QA.

CI/CD with GitHub Actions

GitHub Actions offer a native way to automate build and deployment workflows triggered by GitHub events.

Step 1: Create a GitHub Repository

Push your application code to a public or private GitHub repository.

Step 2: Add a Workflow File

Inside your project, create the following directory and file:

```
.github/workflows/deploy.yml
```

For a Node.js app, a typical GitHub Actions workflow looks like:

```yaml
name: Azure CI/CD

on:
  push:
    branches:
      - main

jobs:
  build-and-deploy:
    runs-on: ubuntu-latest

    steps:
    - name: Checkout code
      uses: actions/checkout@v2

    - name: Set up Node.js
      uses: actions/setup-node@v3
      with:
        node-version: '18'

    - name: Install dependencies
      run: npm install

    - name: Run tests
      run: npm test

    - name: Build app
      run: npm run build

    - name: Deploy to Azure Web App
      uses: azure/webapps-deploy@v2
      with:
```

```
      app-name: 'your-app-name'
      publish-profile: ${{ secrets.AZURE_WEBAPP_PUBLISH_PROFILE }}
      package: .
```

Step 3: Generate and Add Secrets

1. In the Azure Portal, go to your App Service.

2. Click **Get Publish Profile** and download the file.

3. Go to your GitHub repository → **Settings** → **Secrets and variables** → **Actions**.

4. Add a new secret: AZURE_WEBAPP_PUBLISH_PROFILE.

Step 4: Commit and Push

Push your workflow file to the repository. GitHub Actions will automatically trigger the workflow on every push to the main branch.

Using Environments and Secrets

CI/CD processes often require access to sensitive data such as API keys, tokens, and credentials.

- **Azure DevOps**: Use **Library > Variable groups** and mark sensitive variables as secrets.

- **GitHub Actions**: Use **Secrets** in the repository settings.

Example of using a secret in GitHub Actions:

```
env:
  API_KEY: ${{ secrets.MY_API_KEY }}
```

This can be accessed in your scripts with process.env.API_KEY.

CI/CD Best Practices

1. **Keep Pipelines in Version Control**: Store pipeline configurations (`yaml` files) in the repository.

2. **Build Once, Deploy Many**: Avoid rebuilding code separately for each environment.

3. **Use Staging Environments**: Test builds in a staging environment before production.

4. **Enable Rollbacks**: Keep deployment history and versioned builds for easy rollbacks.

5. **Integrate Automated Tests**: Include unit and integration tests in your pipeline.

6. **Fail Fast**: Fail the pipeline early if critical stages (e.g., build or test) fail.

7. **Minimize Secrets Exposure**: Use environment secrets and keep them encrypted.

8. **Use Status Badges**: Add build status badges to your README for visibility.

Monitoring and Alerts

You can monitor build and deployment activity using:

- **Azure DevOps Dashboards**: Track pipeline duration, failure rates, and deployment history.

- **GitHub Actions Insights**: Monitor workflow run times and failures.

- **Azure Monitor and Application Insights**: Observe app health post-deployment.

You can also integrate Slack, Teams, or email alerts for deployment events.

Troubleshooting Common Issues

Build Failures

- Ensure the correct SDK version is used (Node, .NET, Python).

- Validate your `package.json`, `csproj`, or build config files.

Deployment Failures

- Confirm the Azure publish profile is correctly configured.

- Check deployment logs in the Azure Portal under **Deployment Center > Logs**.

Secret Not Found

- Make sure the secret is correctly named and exists in the correct scope (GitHub repo, DevOps project).

Summary

Implementing CI/CD pipelines with Azure empowers developers to ship updates faster and with greater confidence. Azure DevOps Pipelines and GitHub Actions both offer reliable, scalable automation, integrated deeply with Azure services. Whether you're deploying to App Services, Functions, or Containers, these tools help automate every step of your development lifecycle—from code commit to production deployment—ensuring stability, repeatability, and rapid feedback at every stage.

Working with Azure DevOps

Azure DevOps is a comprehensive suite of development tools provided by Microsoft to support the entire software development lifecycle. It provides capabilities for project planning, source control, build automation, release management, and continuous integration/continuous delivery (CI/CD). Whether you're building a small application or managing a complex enterprise system, Azure DevOps offers powerful integrations and extensibility to meet diverse project needs.

This section covers setting up Azure DevOps for development teams, managing source code, configuring build and release pipelines, using boards for agile project management, testing strategies, and best practices for DevOps workflows.

Getting Started with Azure DevOps

To start working with Azure DevOps:

1. Go to https://dev.azure.com and sign in with your Microsoft account.

2. Create a new **Organization**. This acts as a container for multiple projects.

3. Create a **Project** within the organization. You can choose visibility (public or private) and select version control (Git or Team Foundation Version Control - TFVC).

Each project includes the following major services:

- **Boards**: For agile planning and tracking work.

- **Repos**: Git-based source control.

- **Pipelines**: Build and release automation.

- **Test Plans**: Manual and exploratory testing.

- **Artifacts**: Package management (NuGet, npm, Maven).

Using Azure Repos for Source Control

Azure Repos provides Git repositories for source code management. It supports pull requests, branch policies, and integrations with IDEs like Visual Studio and VS Code.

Cloning a Repository

To clone a repository locally:

```
git clone https://dev.azure.com/{organization}/{project}/_git/{repo-name}
```

You can authenticate using a Personal Access Token (PAT) or Azure CLI.

Creating a Branch

Use branching to work on new features independently:

```
git checkout -b feature/add-user-login
```

Push the branch to the remote repo:

```
git push origin feature/add-user-login
```

Creating and Reviewing Pull Requests

Pull requests (PRs) enable peer review before changes are merged.

1. In Azure DevOps, go to **Repos > Pull Requests**.

2. Click **New Pull Request**.

3. Select the source and target branches.

4. Add reviewers and comments.

Pull requests can enforce **branch policies**:

- Require code reviewers.

- Enforce linked work items.

- Require successful builds before merging.

Using Azure Boards for Agile Project Management

Azure Boards helps teams plan, track, and discuss work across the entire development lifecycle using agile tools like Kanban boards, backlogs, and sprint planning.

Work Items

Azure Boards organizes work into items:

- **Epic**: Large bodies of work.

- **Feature**: Groups of user stories.

- **User Story / Task**: Specific functionality or work.

- **Bug**: Issue or defect.

Work items are customizable and can be linked to commits, branches, pull requests, and builds.

Sprint Planning

Use **Iterations** to define sprints. Configure sprint cadence (e.g., every 2 weeks) in **Project Settings > Project Configuration > Iterations**.

Assign work items to sprints, estimate effort using story points, and track progress via burn-down charts and dashboards.

Creating and Configuring Build Pipelines

Azure Pipelines allow automation of builds and tests, triggered on commits, PRs, or schedules.

Creating a YAML Pipeline

1. Navigate to **Pipelines > Pipelines**, then click **New pipeline**.

2. Choose the repository.

3. Select **YAML**.

4. Create a file named `azure-pipelines.yml` in your repo.

Example for a .NET app:

```yaml
trigger:
  branches:
    include:
      - main

pool:
  vmImage: 'windows-latest'

variables:
  buildConfiguration: 'Release'

steps:
- task: UseDotNet@2
  inputs:
    packageType: 'sdk'
    version: '7.0.x'
    installationPath: $(Agent.ToolsDirectory)/dotnet

- script: dotnet build --configuration $(buildConfiguration)
  displayName: 'Build the application'

- script: dotnet test --no-build --verbosity normal
  displayName: 'Run tests'
```

Build Artifacts

Pipelines can generate artifacts for deployment:

```
- task: PublishBuildArtifacts@1
  inputs:
    PathtoPublish: '$(Build.ArtifactStagingDirectory)'
    ArtifactName: 'drop'
```

Artifacts can be used in **Release Pipelines** or downloaded manually.

Creating Release Pipelines for Deployment

Release Pipelines automate deployment of builds to environments such as staging, QA, and production.

Setting Up a Release Pipeline

1. Go to **Pipelines > Releases**.

2. Click **New Pipeline**, add an **Artifact** from a build pipeline.

3. Add a stage and choose a deployment template (e.g., **Azure App Service Deployment**).

4. Configure the environment, app name, and authentication.

Adding Tasks

Tasks define what happens during the deployment. For example:

- Install dependencies

- Run scripts

- Deploy ZIP packages to App Services

- Run database migrations

Release pipelines can include **approvals**, **gates**, and **variables** for control and flexibility.

Testing in Azure DevOps

Azure DevOps supports:

- **Unit testing**: Run tests during the build using frameworks like xUnit, NUnit, or Jest.

- **Code coverage**: Measure how much code is exercised by tests.

- **Test Plans**: Manual test case management.

- **Load Testing (deprecated)**: Now integrated via Azure Load Testing.

Sample .NET Test Step

```
- task: DotNetCoreCLI@2
  inputs:
    command: 'test'
    projects: '**/*.csproj'
    arguments: '--configuration $(buildConfiguration) --collect:"Code Coverage"'
```

Test results are displayed in the **Tests** tab of the pipeline.

Managing Secrets and Variables

Use **Library > Variable Groups** to store and manage secrets:

- Mark variables as secret (encrypted).

- Link groups to pipelines.

- Use environment-specific values.

In pipelines:

```
variables:
  - group: MySecretsGroup
```

Access with $(mySecret).

Extending Azure DevOps with Marketplace Extensions

Azure DevOps supports extensions via the **Visual Studio Marketplace**. Popular extensions include:

- Slack and Microsoft Teams integrations

- SonarCloud for static code analysis

- Terraform integration

- ServiceNow for change management

DevOps Best Practices

1. **Use Infrastructure as Code (IaC)**: Use Bicep, ARM, or Terraform to define infrastructure.

2. **Adopt Trunk-Based Development**: Use short-lived branches, merge frequently.

3. **Automate Everything**: Builds, tests, security scans, deployments.

4. **Shift Left**: Integrate security and quality early in the pipeline.

5. **Monitor Continuously**: Use Application Insights, Azure Monitor.

6. **Use Feature Flags**: Deploy code separately from feature release.

7. **Review and Retrospect**: Use pipeline analytics to improve efficiency.

Summary

Azure DevOps enables teams to plan, develop, build, test, and deliver software more efficiently. With integrated tools like Boards, Repos, Pipelines, and Test Plans, it supports agile development at scale. Configuring your development workflows through Azure DevOps not only improves collaboration and visibility but also helps automate and standardize quality and deployment practices across the organization. By adopting DevOps principles and utilizing the full Azure DevOps suite, development teams can significantly accelerate delivery while maintaining high standards of quality, security, and stability.

Local Development and Azure Integration

Building cloud-native applications doesn't mean everything must happen in the cloud. Local development environments are critical for productivity, debugging, and rapid iteration. Azure provides a wide range of tools and services that integrate seamlessly with local development environments, allowing developers to build, test, and simulate cloud applications on their local machines before deploying to Azure.

This section explores how to set up your local development environment, use Azure tools like the Azure CLI and Azure SDKs, work with emulators and local runtimes, integrate with services like Azure Functions, Cosmos DB, and Storage, and manage seamless deployment from local to cloud.

Setting Up Your Local Development Environment

To develop Azure-integrated applications locally, you need the right tools installed:

Essential Tools

- **Azure CLI**: Command-line interface for managing Azure resources.

- **Azure PowerShell**: An alternative to the CLI for scripting in PowerShell.

- **Visual Studio Code (VS Code)**: Lightweight, extensible editor with Azure extensions.

- **Azure Functions Core Tools**: Local development and testing of serverless apps.

- **Azure Storage Emulator or Azurite**: Local simulation of Blob, Queue, and Table services.

- **.NET SDK / Node.js / Python / Java**: Depending on your application's language.

Installing Azure CLI

```
# On macOS
brew install azure-cli

# On Windows (PowerShell)
Invoke-WebRequest -Uri https://aka.ms/installazurecliwindows -
OutFile .\AzureCLI.msi; Start-Process .\AzureCLI.msi

# On Ubuntu
curl -sL https://aka.ms/InstallAzureCLIDeb | sudo bash
```

Once installed, login with:

```
az login
```

This opens a browser window to authenticate your session.

Using Visual Studio Code with Azure Extensions

VS Code provides first-class integration with Azure through a variety of extensions:

- **Azure Account**: Sign in and manage subscriptions.

- **Azure App Service**: Manage and deploy web apps.

- **Azure Functions**: Develop and deploy serverless functions.

- **Azure Storage**: Access Blob, Queue, and Table storage.

- **Azure Cosmos DB**: Connect to and manage Cosmos DB instances.

You can install these from the VS Code Marketplace or directly via the Extensions tab.

Developing Azure Functions Locally

Azure Functions allow you to build event-driven, serverless applications. You can develop and run them locally using **Azure Functions Core Tools**.

Step 1: Install Core Tools

```
npm install -g azure-functions-core-tools@4 --unsafe-perm true
```

Step 2: Create a Function App

```
func init MyFunctionApp --worker-runtime node
cd MyFunctionApp
func new --name HttpExample --template "HTTP trigger"
```

Step 3: Run the Function Locally

```
func start
```

This starts a local server (typically on http://localhost:7071) where you can test your function.

Step 4: Deploy to Azure

```
func azure functionapp publish <YourAppName>
```

You can also use VS Code to deploy with the **Deploy to Function App** command from the command palette.

Simulating Azure Storage Locally with Azurite

For applications that use Azure Storage (Blob, Table, Queue), you can use **Azurite**, a lightweight emulator.

Install Azurite

```
npm install -g azurite
```

Start Azurite

```
azurite --silent --location ./azurite --debug ./azurite/debug.log
```

Azurite will expose local endpoints:

- Blob service: `http://127.0.0.1:10000`

- Queue service: `http://127.0.0.1:10001`

- Table service: `http://127.0.0.1:10002`

Using Azurite in Code (Node.js Example)

```
const { BlobServiceClient } = require('@azure/storage-blob');
const connectionString = "UseDevelopmentStorage=true";
const blobServiceClient =
BlobServiceClient.fromConnectionString(connectionString);
```

You can use the same APIs as production services with a local connection string.

Local Development with Cosmos DB Emulator

For NoSQL or multi-model data scenarios, Cosmos DB Emulator provides a way to simulate Cosmos DB locally.

Download the Emulator

- Available for Windows from the official Azure Cosmos DB Emulator page.

Default Connection String

```
AccountEndpoint=https://localhost:8081/;AccountKey=C2y6yDjf5/R+ob0N8
A7Cgv30VRJBrCL+...
```

Use this in your application to connect to the local instance.

Debugging Azure Applications Locally

VS Code provides deep integration for debugging:

- Set breakpoints in Functions or Web Apps.

- Attach the debugger to local or remote processes.

- Use integrated terminals for Azure CLI commands.

Example: Debug Azure Function in VS Code

1. Add breakpoints in your code.

2. Press F5 or select **Run > Start Debugging**.

3. Use tools like Postman or `curl` to invoke the function.

Managing Azure Resources from Local Environment

You can create and manage Azure resources from your terminal or scripts using Azure CLI.

Create a Resource Group

```
az group create --name dev-resources --location "East US"
```

Create a Storage Account

```
az storage account create --name mystorageaccount --resource-group
dev-resources --location "East US" --sku Standard_LRS
```

List Web Apps

```
az webapp list --output table
```

Azure CLI also supports scripting and automation via shell scripts or PowerShell.

Using GitHub Codespaces and Dev Containers

For more portable environments, GitHub Codespaces and Dev Containers allow you to define a reproducible development environment using a `.devcontainer` file.

Example `.devcontainer/devcontainer.json`:

```
{
  "name": "Azure Dev Env",
  "image": "mcr.microsoft.com/vscode/devcontainers/javascript-node",
  "features": {
    "ghcr.io/devcontainers/features/azure-cli:1": {}
  }
}
```

You can develop in the cloud or locally using the same containerized environment.

Local-to-Cloud Deployment Workflows

There are multiple options to deploy from local to Azure:

1. Azure CLI

```
az webapp up --name mywebapp --resource-group dev-resources --runtime "NODE|18-lts"
```

This command creates and deploys a local Node.js app to App Service.

2. Git Push Deploy

Enable Git deployment for your App Service:

```
az webapp deployment source config-local-git --name mywebapp --resource-group dev-resources
```

Then push code:

```
git remote add azure https://<app-url>.scm.azurewebsites.net/mywebapp.git
```

```
git push azure main
```

3. Visual Studio Code Deployment

1. Right-click your app folder.

2. Choose **Deploy to Web App**.

3. Select an existing App Service or create a new one.

Best Practices for Local Development with Azure

- **Use Environment Variables**: Avoid hard-coding Azure credentials.

- **Use .env files** for managing local secrets and use libraries like dotenv.

- **Use Azurite and Emulators** when possible to avoid incurring cloud costs.

- **Use Feature Flags** to enable/disable cloud-specific features in local builds.

- **Keep Infrastructure as Code (IaC)** definitions (ARM, Bicep, Terraform) in your project.

- **Simulate Production Environment** locally to avoid integration surprises.

- **Use Linting and Formatters** to maintain code quality.

- **Enable Auto-reload** for faster iteration during development.

Summary

Local development remains an essential part of the modern cloud-based application lifecycle. Azure offers comprehensive support for building, simulating, and testing applications locally while maintaining consistency with cloud environments. From Azure CLI and emulators to integrated deployment via Visual Studio Code and Git, developers can create seamless and productive workflows that bridge local environments and Azure cloud services. Embracing local development best practices ensures faster feedback, reduced costs, and higher confidence in deployments to staging and production.

Chapter 6: Databases and Data Services

Azure SQL Database Basics

Azure SQL Database is a fully managed platform-as-a-service (PaaS) database engine designed to handle most database management functions such as upgrading, patching, backups, and monitoring without user involvement. It provides high availability, performance tuning, and scalability out-of-the-box, making it an optimal solution for cloud-native applications as well as existing applications being migrated to the cloud.

Understanding Azure SQL Database

Azure SQL Database is based on the latest stable version of Microsoft SQL Server Database Engine. It comes with built-in features like high availability, backups, and scaling, which allows developers to focus on building applications without worrying about the infrastructure layer.

There are two primary deployment models:

- **Single Database**: A fully managed isolated database suitable for modern cloud applications that require performance guarantees.

- **Elastic Pool**: A collection of databases with a shared set of resources such as CPU and memory. Ideal for SaaS applications with multiple databases that have varying usage patterns.

Key Features

- **Managed Backups**: Automatic backups with configurable retention periods.

- **Dynamic Scalability**: Easily scale compute and storage resources with minimal downtime.

- **Geo-replication**: Built-in support for replicating databases to other Azure regions.

- **Advanced Security**: Built-in features like threat detection, encryption at rest, and auditing.

Creating an Azure SQL Database

You can create an Azure SQL Database using the Azure Portal, Azure CLI, ARM templates, or PowerShell.

Here's how to create one using the Azure CLI:

```
# Create a resource group
az group create --name MyResourceGroup --location eastus

# Create a logical SQL server
az sql server create \
  --name my-sql-server \
  --resource-group MyResourceGroup \
  --location eastus \
  --admin-user adminuser \
  --admin-password StrongPassword123!

# Create a SQL database
az sql db create \
  --resource-group MyResourceGroup \
  --server my-sql-server \
  --name mySampleDatabase \
  --service-objective S0
```

Connecting to Your Database

Once the database is created, you can connect to it using tools like SQL Server Management Studio (SSMS), Azure Data Studio, or programmatically using connection strings.

Sample ADO.NET connection string:

```
string connectionString = "Server=tcp:my-sql-
server.database.windows.net,1433;Initial
Catalog=mySampleDatabase;Persist Security Info=False;User.
ID=adminuser;Password=StrongPassword123!;MultipleActiveResultSets=Fa
lse;Encrypt=True;TrustServerCertificate=False;Connection
Timeout=30;";
```

You must configure the server-level firewall rules to allow client IP addresses to connect.

Performance Tiers and Purchasing Models

Azure SQL Database supports various service tiers that are divided into two purchasing models:

- **DTU-based model**: Database Transaction Units (DTUs) represent a blended measure of CPU, memory, and read/write rates.

- **vCore-based model**: Offers more transparency and flexibility in terms of compute, memory, and IO resources.

Choosing between these models depends on workload predictability and control requirements.

Feature	DTU Model	vCore Model
Simplicity	Easier to use	More control
Transparency	Less transparent	Full resource control
Customization	Limited	High

Security Best Practices

- **Use Active Directory Authentication**: This allows centralized user management and integration with Azure RBAC.

- **Enable Transparent Data Encryption (TDE)**: This is enabled by default and encrypts the storage associated with the database.

- **Use Always Encrypted**: This protects sensitive data, ensuring data is encrypted in use and only accessible by authorized clients.

```
-- Example of encrypting a column using Always Encrypted
CREATE TABLE Customers (
    CustomerID INT PRIMARY KEY,
    FirstName NVARCHAR(50) COLLATE Latin1_General_BIN2 ENCRYPTED
WITH (
        COLUMN_ENCRYPTION_KEY = MyCEK,
        ENCRYPTION_TYPE = DETERMINISTIC,
        ALGORITHM = 'AEAD_AES_256_CBC_HMAC_SHA_256'
    )
);
```

Automatic Tuning

Azure SQL Database can automatically apply performance tuning recommendations to improve query performance and index management:

- **Automatic Index Management**: Automatically creates or drops indexes based on usage.

- **Query Performance Insight**: Provides in-depth analysis of query performance.

Enable automatic tuning:

```
az sql db automatic-tuning update \
  --resource-group MyResourceGroup \
  --server my-sql-server \
  --name mySampleDatabase \
  --desired-state Auto
```

Monitoring and Alerts

Monitoring your Azure SQL Database is essential for maintaining performance and availability. Azure provides several tools:

- **Azure Monitor**: Offers metrics such as CPU usage, DTU usage, and storage consumption.

- **SQL Analytics (in Log Analytics workspace)**: Allows you to analyze database performance across your environment.

- **Alerts**: Set up alerts based on metrics to receive notifications or trigger actions.

```
az monitor metrics alert create \
  --name "HighDTUUsageAlert" \
  --resource-group MyResourceGroup \
  --scopes /subscriptions/{subscription-
id}/resourceGroups/MyResourceGroup/providers/Microsoft.Sql/servers/m
y-sql-server/databases/mySampleDatabase \
  --condition "avg dtu_consumption_percent > 80" \
  --description "DTU usage is over 80%" \
  --action-group MyActionGroup
```

High Availability and Disaster Recovery

Azure SQL Database offers a 99.99% uptime SLA. Key availability features include:

- **Zone Redundant Deployments**: Databases are replicated across multiple availability zones.

- **Active Geo-Replication**: Allows creating readable secondary databases in different regions.

- **Failover Groups**: Automatically fail over databases in case of a regional outage.

Set up Geo-Replication:

```
az sql db replica create \
  --name mySampleDatabase \
  --resource-group MyResourceGroup \
  --server my-sql-server \
  --partner-server my-secondary-server \
  --partner-resource-group MySecondaryRG \
  --elastic-pool myElasticPool
```

Backup and Restore

Automatic backups are enabled by default and retained for 7 to 35 days depending on the pricing tier. You can also perform long-term retention.

Restoring a deleted database:

```
az sql db restore \
  --dest-name myRestoredDatabase \
  --deleted-time "2023-12-01T00:00:00Z" \
  --name mySampleDatabase \
  --resource-group MyResourceGroup \
  --server my-sql-server
```

Use long-term retention to retain backups for up to 10 years:

```
az sql db ltr-policy set \
  --name mySampleDatabase \
  --resource-group MyResourceGroup \
  --server my-sql-server \
  --weekly-retention P12W
```

Migration to Azure SQL Database

You can migrate existing SQL Server workloads to Azure SQL Database using the **Azure Database Migration Service (DMS)** or **Data Migration Assistant (DMA)**.

Steps include:

1. Assess your on-premises database with DMA.

2. Choose the appropriate Azure SQL Database service tier.

3. Use DMS to perform the migration.

4. Validate data and cut over production workloads.

Use Cases

- **Enterprise Applications**: Store and process transactional data for business applications.

- **Web Applications**: Backend database for ASP.NET, Java, or Node.js applications hosted on Azure App Services.

- **Data Analytics**: Serve as a source for analytics pipelines or integrations with Power BI.

By leveraging the full capabilities of Azure SQL Database, developers and database administrators can achieve a secure, highly available, and scalable solution with minimal overhead. This managed service enables rapid application development while ensuring robust data storage, security, and operational continuity.

Working with Cosmos DB

Azure Cosmos DB is Microsoft's globally distributed, multi-model database service designed to provide high availability, low latency, and scalability for mission-critical applications. As a PaaS offering, Cosmos DB abstracts much of the underlying infrastructure complexity while offering a rich set of APIs for developers to use, including SQL (Core), MongoDB, Cassandra, Gremlin, and Table APIs.

Cosmos DB is built for high throughput and low latency at global scale. It enables developers to write responsive, scalable applications that need to serve users around the world while maintaining data consistency, availability, and partitioning.

Core Concepts of Cosmos DB

Before diving into development, it's essential to understand the core architectural concepts of Cosmos DB:

- **Database Account**: The top-level resource, unique for each region and account.

- **Database**: A container for collections (SQL API) or other model-specific containers.

- **Container**: A schema-agnostic entity for storing JSON documents, graphs, or key-value pairs depending on the API.

- **Item**: The individual record or entity within a container.

- **Partition Key**: Used to distribute data and ensure scalability and performance.

- **Throughput (RU/s)**: Request Units per second – a currency model for measuring the performance load and billing.

APIs and Data Models

Cosmos DB supports multiple APIs to allow flexibility in how you structure and interact with data:

- **SQL (Core)**: JSON document model with SQL-like query language.

- **MongoDB API**: Enables existing MongoDB client applications to use Cosmos DB.

- **Cassandra API**: Use Cassandra SDKs to connect with Cosmos DB.

- **Gremlin API**: Graph-based queries for traversal and relationship analysis.

- **Table API**: For key-value store use cases similar to Azure Table Storage.

For the purpose of this section, we will primarily focus on the SQL API.

Creating a Cosmos DB Account and SQL Container

You can create a Cosmos DB SQL API instance using the Azure Portal, ARM, PowerShell, or Azure CLI.

```
# Create a resource group
az group create --name cosmos-rg --location westus

# Create Cosmos DB account
az cosmosdb create \
  --name my-cosmos-account \
```

```
  --resource-group cosmos-rg \
  --kind GlobalDocumentDB \
  --locations regionName=westus failoverPriority=0
isZoneRedundant=false

# Create a database
az cosmosdb sql database create \
  --account-name my-cosmos-account \
  --resource-group cosmos-rg \
  --name my-database

# Create a container with partition key
az cosmosdb sql container create \
  --account-name my-cosmos-account \
  --resource-group cosmos-rg \
  --database-name my-database \
  --name my-container \
  --partition-key-path "/userId" \
  --throughput 400
```

Understanding Partitioning and Throughput

Partitioning enables Cosmos DB to scale horizontally by distributing data across multiple physical partitions. Choosing the right partition key is critical for performance and scalability.

Best practices:

- Choose a partition key with high cardinality.

- Ensure a balanced distribution of request load.

- Avoid hot partitions.

Throughput is provisioned in **Request Units per second (RU/s)**, which abstracts CPU, IO, and memory. All operations, such as reads and writes, consume RUs.

For example:

- A simple read may cost ~1 RU.

- A document write can cost between 5–20 RUs depending on the size and indexing.

You can configure **manual** or **autoscale throughput**. Autoscale adjusts throughput based on the workload within a defined range (e.g., 400–4000 RU/s).

Working with Data: Insert, Query, and Update

Here's a sample JSON document stored in Cosmos DB:

```json
{
  "id": "1",
  "userId": "u123",
  "name": "Alice Johnson",
  "email": "alice@example.com",
  "joined": "2025-01-15T08:00:00Z"
}
```

Using the Azure Cosmos DB SDK for Node.js, you can perform CRUD operations as follows:

Installation

```
npm install @azure/cosmos
```

Connecting to Cosmos DB

```javascript
const { CosmosClient } = require("@azure/cosmos");

const endpoint = "https://my-cosmos-account.documents.azure.com:443/";
const key = "your-primary-key";

const client = new CosmosClient({ endpoint, key });

const database = client.database("my-database");
const container = database.container("my-container");
```

Inserting a Document

```javascript
const newItem = {
  id: "2",
  userId: "u124",
  name: "Bob Smith",
  email: "bob@example.com",
  joined: new Date().toISOString()
};
```

```javascript
const { resource: createdItem } = await
container.items.create(newItem);
console.log(`Created item: ${createdItem.id}`);
```

Querying Documents
```javascript
const querySpec = {
  query: "SELECT * FROM c WHERE c.userId = @userId",
  parameters: [
    { name: "@userId", value: "u123" }
  ]
};

const { resources: results } = await
container.items.query(querySpec).fetchAll();
results.forEach(item => console.log(item));
```

Updating a Document
```javascript
const { resource: item } = await container.item("1", "u123").read();
item.email = "alice.johnson@newdomain.com";
await container.item("1", "u123").replace(item);
```

Deleting a Document
```javascript
await container.item("2", "u124").delete();
console.log("Deleted item with id 2");
```

Indexing in Cosmos DB

Cosmos DB automatically indexes all properties by default. This makes queries fast without requiring manual index management. However, you can define custom indexing policies to optimize performance and reduce RU consumption.

Example of a custom indexing policy:

```json
{
  "indexingMode": "consistent",
  "includedPaths": [
    {
      "path": "/name/?"
    },
    {
```

```
      "path": "/email/?"
    }
  ],
  "excludedPaths": [
    {
      "path": "/*"
    }
  ]
}
```

Consistency Models

Cosmos DB offers five well-defined consistency levels:

1. **Strong**: Linearizability. Most consistent, least available.

2. **Bounded Staleness**: Lag defined by time or versions.

3. **Session** (default): Guarantees consistency for a single session.

4. **Consistent Prefix**: Reads never see out-of-order writes.

5. **Eventual**: Least consistent, most available.

Choose a consistency level based on the trade-off between latency, availability, and data integrity for your use case.

Global Distribution

One of Cosmos DB's flagship features is global distribution. With just a few clicks or a single CLI command, you can replicate your database across any of Azure's regions.

Benefits:

- Low latency reads/writes for globally distributed users.

- Automatic multi-region failover.

- Data sovereignty and compliance.

```
az cosmosdb update \
  --name my-cosmos-account \
  --resource-group cosmos-rg \
```

```
--locations regionName=eastus2 failoverPriority=1
isZoneRedundant=false
```

Backup and Restore

Cosmos DB provides automatic backups with a 30-day retention by default. Point-in-time restore can be used to recover a container or entire database.

Long-term backup is managed through **Azure Backup** or **Change Feed**, which captures a continuous log of changes.

Change Feed

The **Change Feed** enables you to listen to inserts and updates in real time. Ideal for event-driven architectures and data pipelines.

```
const iterator = container.items.changeFeed().getAsyncIterator();
for await (const item of iterator) {
  console.log("Detected change: ", item);
}
```

This allows for real-time syncing with Azure Functions, Logic Apps, or even Kafka producers.

Security and Compliance

Cosmos DB supports enterprise-grade security out of the box:

- **Network Isolation**: Use private endpoints to restrict access.

- **IP Firewall**: Allow access only from specific IP ranges.

- **Role-Based Access Control (RBAC)**: Fine-grained access controls using Azure AD.

- **Encryption**: Data is encrypted at rest with Microsoft-managed keys or customer-managed keys.

```
az cosmosdb update \
  --name my-cosmos-account \
  --resource-group cosmos-rg \
  --enable-virtual-network true
```

Integration with Other Azure Services

Cosmos DB integrates seamlessly with many Azure services:

- **Azure Functions**: Real-time triggers on Change Feed.

- **Azure Synapse Analytics**: For large-scale data analytics.

- **Power BI**: Direct connectivity for visualization.

- **Logic Apps**: Automate workflows based on data changes.

Use Cases

- **IoT Applications**: Handle massive volumes of sensor data with low-latency writes.

- **Personalized User Experiences**: Store user profiles and preferences globally.

- **Real-time Recommendation Engines**: Use fast queries and Change Feed to drive suggestions.

- **Multi-tenant SaaS Platforms**: Separate customer data using partition keys.

Azure Cosmos DB is a powerful choice for modern cloud-native applications that need global distribution, scalability, low latency, and multi-model flexibility. With a range of APIs, built-in consistency levels, and rich tooling, Cosmos DB enables developers to deliver robust and responsive data services with ease.

NoSQL and Table Storage Use Cases

Azure offers a variety of NoSQL storage options tailored for different use cases. Among these, Azure Table Storage stands out as a cost-effective, scalable, and schema-less storage solution ideal for semi-structured and non-relational data. In this section, we will explore what Table Storage is, how it compares with other NoSQL options like Cosmos DB and Azure Blob Storage, and look at various real-world use cases where NoSQL and Table Storage excel.

Overview of NoSQL on Azure

NoSQL databases differ from traditional relational databases by offering more flexibility in how data is stored and queried. They are designed for performance, scalability, and availability in cloud environments. Azure supports several NoSQL storage models:

- **Key-Value Stores** (e.g., Azure Table Storage)

- **Document Stores** (e.g., Cosmos DB with SQL or MongoDB API)

- **Wide Column Stores** (e.g., Cosmos DB with Cassandra API)

- **Graph Databases** (e.g., Cosmos DB with Gremlin API)

Azure Table Storage is part of the Azure Storage account and offers a straightforward way to store and retrieve large amounts of structured data. Each record in a table is called an **entity**, similar to a row in relational databases. Entities contain properties, which are name-value pairs.

Key Concepts of Table Storage

- **Storage Account**: The container for all Azure Storage services.

- **Table**: The collection of entities.

- **Entity**: A single row of data.

- **PartitionKey**: Used to group related entities and enables scalable queries.

- **RowKey**: The unique identifier for an entity within a partition.

- **Timestamp**: A system-generated property used for concurrency.

An entity is identified uniquely by a combination of PartitionKey and RowKey.

Example entity:

```
{
  "PartitionKey": "Customer",
  "RowKey": "C001",
  "Name": "Emily Taylor",
  "Email": "emily.taylor@example.com",
  "CreatedDate": "2025-04-05T12:00:00Z"
}
```

Table Storage vs. Cosmos DB Table API

Feature	Azure Table Storage	Cosmos DB Table API
Throughput	Standard, limited to storage performance	High, auto-scalable RU/s

Global Distribution	No	Yes
SLA	99.9%	99.999%
Cost	Lower	Higher, but more features
Latency	Higher	Lower
Consistency Models	Eventual	Multiple levels

If your application needs low-latency, global access, and scaling, Cosmos DB Table API is a better choice. For cost-sensitive apps with less complex access patterns, Table Storage is ideal.

Creating and Accessing Table Storage

You can use the Azure Portal, Azure CLI, PowerShell, or SDKs to create and manage Table Storage.

```
# Create a storage account
az storage account create \
  --name mystorageacct \
  --resource-group mystorage-rg \
  --location eastus \
  --sku Standard_LRS

# Create a table
az storage table create \
  --name customerdata \
  --account-name mystorageacct
```

Working with the Azure SDK

To interact with Table Storage in code, use the Azure SDK. Here's how to get started with Node.js:

Install SDK

```
npm install @azure/data-tables
```

Connect and Insert Data

```
const { TableClient, AzureNamedKeyCredential } =
require("@azure/data-tables");

const account = "mystorageacct";
const accountKey = "your_storage_account_key";
const tableName = "customerdata";

const credential = new AzureNamedKeyCredential(account, accountKey);
const client = new
TableClient(`https://${account}.table.core.windows.net`, tableName,
credential);

async function insertEntity() {
  const entity = {
    partitionKey: "Customer",
    rowKey: "C001",
    name: "Emily Taylor",
    email: "emily.taylor@example.com",
    createdDate: new Date().toISOString()
  };

  await client.createEntity(entity);
  console.log("Entity inserted.");
}
```

Querying Entities

```
async function queryEntity() {
  const entities = client.listEntities({
    queryOptions: {
      filter: "PartitionKey eq 'Customer'"
    }
  });

  for await (const entity of entities) {
    console.log(entity);
  }
}
```

Updating and Deleting

```
async function updateEntity() {
```

```
  const updated = {
    partitionKey: "Customer",
    rowKey: "C001",
    email: "emily.taylor@newdomain.com"
  };

  await client.updateEntity(updated, "Merge");
}

async function deleteEntity() {
  await client.deleteEntity("Customer", "C001");
}
```

Use Cases for NoSQL and Table Storage

1. User Profiles and Preferences

Applications often need to store user profiles, settings, and preferences in a scalable manner. Table Storage allows schema-less storage, so each user can have unique sets of preferences.

```
{
  "PartitionKey": "UserProfile",
  "RowKey": "U123",
  "Username": "techgeek",
  "Theme": "dark",
  "NotificationsEnabled": true
}
```

This structure can easily be extended for additional preferences without altering an existing schema.

2. Audit Logs

You can record and query audit trails of user actions or system events using time-based RowKey values. Partition by user or system component, and use timestamps for sorting.

```
{
  "PartitionKey": "SystemX",
  "RowKey": "20250407120000",
  "Action": "FileUploaded",
  "Username": "admin",
  "Filename": "report.pdf"
```

```
}
```

This enables fast querying by date ranges or user.

3. IoT Device Data

IoT applications often ingest high volumes of data that need to be stored quickly. Table Storage is ideal for storing time-series data with minimal schema constraints.

```
{

  "PartitionKey": "Device123",
  "RowKey": "20250407123000",
  "Temperature": 21.3,
  "Humidity": 45.6,
  "Status": "Normal"
}
```

You can partition by device ID and use timestamp-based RowKeys for time-ordered data ingestion.

4. E-Commerce Catalogs

For simple product listings and metadata where relational integrity is not critical, Table Storage can serve as a fast backend store.

```
{

  "PartitionKey": "Electronics",
  "RowKey": "SKU12345",
  "Name": "Wireless Mouse",
  "Price": 29.99,
  "Stock": 150
}
```

It's easy to scale and query based on category, SKU, or other indexed fields.

5. Feature Flags and Configuration

Table Storage can be used to implement lightweight feature flag systems or app configuration settings per environment or customer.

```
{

  "PartitionKey": "FeatureFlags",
  "RowKey": "BetaFeatureX",
  "IsEnabled": true,
```

```
    "TargetUserGroup": "InternalTesters"
}
```

Applications can quickly query flags at startup or on demand to determine enabled features.

Best Practices for Table Storage

- **Design for Partitioning**: Choose a `PartitionKey` that distributes load evenly and scales with your application.

- **Avoid Hot Partitions**: Don't use static PartitionKeys for large volumes of concurrent operations.

- **Batch Operations**: Group insert/update operations per partition to reduce network round trips.

- **Data Modeling**: Use denormalized structures; join operations are not supported.

- **Indexing**: Only PartitionKey and RowKey are indexed. Plan your queries accordingly.

Security and Access Control

Azure Storage uses Shared Key, Shared Access Signatures (SAS), and Azure AD for authentication.

Generate a SAS token for restricted access:

```
az storage account generate-sas \
  --account-name mystorageacct \
  --permissions rwdlacup \
  --services t \
  --resource-types sco \
  --expiry 2025-12-31T23:59:00Z \
  --output tsv
```

You can also enforce secure transfer and use private endpoints for enhanced network isolation.

Backup and Disaster Recovery

While Azure Table Storage does not offer native backup and restore features like Azure SQL or Cosmos DB, you can implement your own using:

- **Azure Functions**: Periodically export data to Blob Storage.

- **Azure Data Factory**: Extract and store snapshots.

- **Change tracking**: Via manual implementation or third-party tools.

Integration and Extensibility

Table Storage integrates well with other Azure services:

- **Azure Functions**: Trigger on new data writes or periodically read tables.

- **Logic Apps**: Read and write to tables as part of automation flows.

- **Power BI**: Pull data using connectors and transform using Power Query.

- **Azure Synapse**: Load data into SQL pools for analytics.

Conclusion

Azure Table Storage and other NoSQL models provide powerful, flexible, and cost-effective data solutions for a wide range of cloud applications. With proper partitioning, lightweight schema management, and simple API interactions, you can build high-performance apps that scale with user demand and handle massive volumes of data.

While Table Storage may not offer advanced features like global replication or fine-grained indexing, it serves many production scenarios well—especially when simplicity, speed, and affordability are top priorities. Understanding the strengths and constraints of Azure's NoSQL offerings helps ensure you pick the right solution for your specific business needs.

Data Security and Backup Strategies

Data is one of the most valuable assets in any application, and securing that data along with implementing robust backup strategies is a foundational part of any cloud-based solution. In Microsoft Azure, a wide range of security features and backup services are available to help developers and organizations ensure data integrity, compliance, availability, and protection against threats or accidental loss.

This section explores how to effectively secure your databases and storage services and set up reliable, scalable backup mechanisms across different Azure data services like Azure SQL Database, Cosmos DB, and Azure Storage (including Table and Blob Storage).

Principles of Data Security in Azure

Azure's approach to data security is built upon the principles of **Defense in Depth** and **Zero Trust**. These are enforced through:

- **Identity and Access Management**

- **Encryption at Rest and in Transit**

- **Network Security Controls**

- **Advanced Threat Protection**

- **Monitoring and Auditing**

Together, these ensure that data is protected from unauthorized access, malicious attacks, data leaks, and misconfigurations.

Securing Azure SQL Database

Azure SQL Database is a PaaS offering with built-in security capabilities. Key security mechanisms include:

1. Authentication and Authorization

- **SQL Authentication**: Uses username and password. Simple to use but less secure.

- **Azure AD Authentication**: Integrates with Azure Active Directory for centralized identity and access management. Supports MFA and RBAC.

```
-- Example: Create a contained user mapped to Azure AD
CREATE USER [user@domain.com] FROM EXTERNAL PROVIDER;
ALTER ROLE db_datareader ADD MEMBER [user@domain.com];
```

2. Firewall Rules

Restrict access to known IP ranges only.

```
az sql server firewall-rule create \
  --resource-group MyResourceGroup \
  --server my-sql-server \
  --name AllowMyOffice \
  --start-ip-address 203.0.113.0 \
  --end-ip-address 203.0.113.255
```

3. Encryption

- **Transparent Data Encryption (TDE)**: Encrypts data at rest. Enabled by default.

- **Always Encrypted**: Protects sensitive data while in use by client-side encryption.

- **TLS Encryption**: Ensures data in transit is encrypted.

4. Threat Detection and Auditing

Azure SQL includes built-in threat detection for identifying anomalous activities like SQL injection, login attempts, and privilege escalations.

Enable auditing:

```
az sql server audit-policy update \
  --resource-group MyResourceGroup \
  --server my-sql-server \
  --state Enabled \
  --blob-storage-target-state Enabled \
  --storage-account myStorageAccount
```

Threat detection alerts can be sent via email or connected to SIEM tools using Azure Monitor.

Securing Cosmos DB

Cosmos DB provides enterprise-grade security features suitable for mission-critical apps.

1. Role-Based Access Control (RBAC)

Assign access at the Azure resource level using Azure AD roles. Roles can be scoped to accounts, databases, or containers.

```
az cosmosdb sql role assignment create \
  --account-name my-cosmos-account \
  --resource-group cosmos-rg \
  --role-definition-id my-role-id \
  --principal-id my-user-object-id \
  --scope "/dbs/my-database/colls/my-container"
```

2. Keys and Connection Strings

Each Cosmos DB account has primary and secondary keys. Rotate keys regularly using automation or Azure Key Vault.

```
az cosmosdb regenerate-key \
  --name my-cosmos-account \
  --resource-group cosmos-rg \
  --key-kind primary
```

3. Private Endpoints

Secure traffic to Cosmos DB over a private Azure Virtual Network.

```
az network private-endpoint create \
  --name cosmosPrivateEndpoint \
  --resource-group cosmos-rg \
  --vnet-name my-vnet \
  --subnet my-subnet \
  --private-connection-resource-id
/subscriptions/.../cosmosdbAccounts/my-cosmos-account \
  --group-ids Sql
```

4. Data Encryption

- **Encryption at Rest**: Enabled by default using Microsoft-managed or customer-managed keys.

- **Encryption in Transit**: All connections require HTTPS.

Securing Azure Storage (Blob, Table, Queue, File)

Azure Storage accounts serve as the foundation for unstructured data, and security must be carefully configured.

1. Shared Access Signatures (SAS)

Grant limited-time, scoped access to storage resources.

```
az storage container generate-sas \
  --account-name mystorageacct \
  --name mycontainer \
  --permissions r \
  --expiry 2025-04-30T23:59Z \
  --output tsv
```

You can restrict access to blobs or tables without exposing the storage account keys.

2. Azure AD Authentication

For enterprise scenarios, use Azure AD identities to authenticate requests and enforce RBAC.

```
az role assignment create \
  --assignee user@domain.com \
  --role "Storage Blob Data Contributor" \
  --scope
"/subscriptions/.../resourceGroups/.../providers/Microsoft.Storage/s
torageAccounts/mystorageacct"
```

3. Storage Firewall and Private Endpoints

Restrict access by IP or force all access through private network paths.

```
az storage account update \
  --name mystorageacct \
  --default-action Deny \
  --bypass AzureServices
```

4. Encryption

- **Encryption at Rest**: Uses AES-256 by default.

- **Client-Side Encryption**: Encrypt data before uploading for extra security.

Backup Strategies Across Azure Data Services

Reliable backups are critical to protect against accidental deletions, corruption, or ransomware.

Azure SQL Database

Backups are managed automatically.

- **Point-in-Time Restore**: Available for 7–35 days depending on tier.

- **Long-Term Retention (LTR)**: Retain weekly/monthly/yearly backups.

```
az sql db ltr-policy set \
  --name myDatabase \
  --resource-group MyResourceGroup \
  --server my-sql-server \
  --weekly-retention P12W \
  --monthly-retention P6M \
  --yearly-retention P5Y \
  --week-of-year 16
```

Restore:

```
az sql db restore \
  --dest-name myDatabaseRestore \
  --deleted-time "2025-04-01T12:00:00Z" \
  --name myDatabase \
  --resource-group MyResourceGroup \
  --server my-sql-server
```

Cosmos DB

Point-in-time restore must be explicitly enabled and is region-specific.

```
az cosmosdb backup-policy update \
  --name my-cosmos-account \
  --resource-group cosmos-rg \
  --backup-policy-type Continuous
```

Restore:

```
az cosmosdb restore \
  --account-name my-cosmos-account \
  --target-account-name restored-cosmos-account \
  --restore-timestamp "2025-04-01T12:00:00Z" \
  --resource-group cosmos-rg \
  --location eastus
```

Azure Blob and File Storage

Use Azure Backup or custom solutions with Azure Functions and Logic Apps.

Enable soft delete:
```
```

```
az storage blob service-properties delete-policy update \
  --account-name mystorageacct \
  --enable true \
  --days-retained 30
```

Azure Table Storage

Azure Table Storage does not have native backup. Use one of the following:

- **Export to Blob using Data Factory**

- **Periodic snapshots via Azure Functions**

- **Scheduled exports with AzCopy**

Example using AzCopy:

```
azcopy copy \
  "https://mystorageacct.table.core.windows.net/mytable?{SAS_TOKEN}" \
  "https://backupstorage.blob.core.windows.net/backups" \
  --recursive
```

Monitoring and Alerting for Security and Backups

Monitoring is vital to detect unauthorized access and backup failures.

- **Azure Monitor**: Track metrics and logs.

- **Azure Policy**: Enforce encryption, firewalls, and backup policies.

- **Azure Security Center**: Unified security management.

- **Alerts**: Notify on suspicious logins, data access anomalies, or backup failures.

Example alert rule:

```
az monitor metrics alert create \
  --name "UnauthorizedAccessAlert" \
  --resource-group MyResourceGroup \
```

```
  --scopes
/subscriptions/.../resourceGroups/.../providers/Microsoft.Sql/server
s/my-sql-server \
  --condition "count > 0" \
  --description "Detects unauthorized access attempts"
```

Final Recommendations

- **Use Azure AD for all authentication**: Where supported, avoid key-based access.

- **Enable soft delete and versioning**: Adds an extra layer of recovery.

- **Encrypt everything**: Use both in-transit and at-rest encryption.

- **Isolate networks**: Use VNETs, private endpoints, and firewall rules.

- **Automate backups**: Regularly export or archive to secondary storage.

- **Test restores**: Periodically validate that backups are restorable.

- **Use Azure Policy**: To enforce security and backup standards across your organization.

With Azure's powerful security and backup capabilities, you can confidently protect your data and applications. By layering best practices across identity, encryption, access control, and monitoring, and implementing backup plans tailored to each service's capabilities, you reduce risk and ensure business continuity in any situation.

Chapter 7: Monitoring, Logging, and Security

Using Azure Monitor and Application Insights

In modern cloud development, ensuring the reliability, performance, and security of your applications requires comprehensive monitoring and diagnostic capabilities. Azure provides developers with a robust set of tools under the Azure Monitor umbrella, which includes Application Insights for deep application-level monitoring and diagnostics.

Azure Monitor and Application Insights help developers and DevOps professionals collect, analyze, and act upon telemetry data from cloud and on-premises environments. These services provide vital visibility into application health, performance bottlenecks, and user behavior, facilitating proactive issue resolution and continuous improvement.

Introduction to Azure Monitor

Azure Monitor is the central monitoring service in Azure, designed to maximize the performance and availability of applications and services. It provides a full-stack monitoring experience, allowing you to observe infrastructure, application, and network layers in a single unified platform.

Key capabilities of Azure Monitor include:

- Metrics collection

- Log analytics

- Alerts and notifications

- Dashboards

- Integration with external tools like Power BI, Grafana, and third-party incident management systems

Azure Monitor works by collecting data from various sources, such as Azure resources, virtual machines, and custom instrumentation within your applications. This data is stored and analyzed to provide actionable insights.

Data Types Collected by Azure Monitor

Azure Monitor collects and organizes data into two fundamental types:

- **Metrics**: Lightweight numerical values collected at regular intervals. Metrics are useful for real-time monitoring and alerting, such as CPU usage, memory consumption, and request rates.

- **Logs**: Structured records of events. Logs provide context and detail, such as error traces, custom events, and audit trails.

You can query this data using **Kusto Query Language (KQL)** in Log Analytics.

Overview of Application Insights

Application Insights is a feature of Azure Monitor that provides Application Performance Monitoring (APM) for developers. It is designed to help you detect issues, diagnose root causes, and understand how your application is used.

With Application Insights, you can monitor:

- Server response times and failure rates

- Dependency tracking (HTTP calls, SQL requests, etc.)

- User interactions and sessions

- Exception reports and stack traces

- Performance counters and custom telemetry

Application Insights supports many development platforms, including .NET, Java, Node.js, Python, and more. You can easily integrate it using SDKs or agent-based instrumentation.

Setting Up Azure Monitor and Application Insights

To get started, you'll typically:

1. **Create an Application Insights resource** via the Azure Portal or CLI.

2. **Install the SDK** in your application.

3. **Configure telemetry collection**, such as request telemetry, dependency tracking, and custom events.

4. **Query and visualize** the data using Log Analytics and dashboards.

Here's an example for a .NET Core web application:

```
dotnet add package Microsoft.ApplicationInsights.AspNetCore
```

In your `Startup.cs` file:

```
public void ConfigureServices(IServiceCollection services)
{
    services.AddApplicationInsightsTelemetry();
}
```

This minimal setup enables automatic collection of telemetry data, which can then be viewed in the Azure Portal under the Application Insights resource.

Using Log Analytics to Query Data

Once your application is sending telemetry data, you can use Log Analytics to query and visualize it. Here's a simple KQL query to view the number of requests by response code:

```
requests
| summarize Count = count() by resultCode
| order by Count desc
```

To identify the slowest operations:

```
requests
| where duration > 500ms
| project name, duration, url, timestamp
| order by duration desc
```

This empowers teams to pinpoint performance bottlenecks and prioritize optimizations.

Creating Alerts

Alerts are essential for proactive monitoring. Azure Monitor allows you to define alert rules based on metrics or log queries.

For example, you can set an alert for when server response time exceeds 1 second:

1. Navigate to your Application Insights resource.

2. Select "Alerts" > "New alert rule".

3. Set the **condition** using the "Server response time" metric.

4. Define **thresholds, frequency**, and **notification actions** (email, webhook, etc.).

5. Review and create the alert.

Alerts can also trigger automation via Logic Apps or Azure Functions.

Custom Telemetry and Events

Application Insights allows you to send custom telemetry, such as business-specific events, user actions, and trace logs.

Example in C#:

```csharp
var telemetry = new TelemetryClient();
telemetry.TrackEvent("UserRegistered",
    new Dictionary<string, string> { { "UserType", "Premium" } },
    new Dictionary<string, double> { { "RegistrationTime", 1.25 }
});
```

This level of customization provides insights specific to your application logic and user experience.

Dashboards and Visualization

You can visualize monitoring data using Azure Dashboards or Power BI. To create a dashboard:

1. Go to the Azure Portal.

2. Select "Dashboard" > "New Dashboard".

3. Use tiles to pin charts from Azure Monitor or Application Insights.

4. Share dashboards with your team for collaborative observability.

Dashboards can include metrics, log charts, availability tests, and alerts, giving you a single-pane view of your application health.

Availability and Performance Testing

Application Insights includes **availability tests** that simulate user traffic to ensure endpoints are responsive and available.

To set one up:

1. In Application Insights, go to "Availability".

2. Add a new test by specifying the URL, frequency, and location.

3. Set success criteria such as response time thresholds and HTTP status codes.

These synthetic checks are critical for identifying outages before users are affected.

Best Practices for Monitoring

To effectively use Azure Monitor and Application Insights:

- **Instrument early and often**: Integrate telemetry during development.

- **Set actionable alerts**: Avoid alert fatigue by targeting meaningful thresholds.

- **Correlate logs and metrics**: Combine views for comprehensive diagnostics.

- **Use sampling**: Manage data volume and cost with smart telemetry sampling.

- **Review and iterate**: Regularly assess your observability strategy and refine telemetry.

Integration with DevOps

Azure Monitor integrates with CI/CD pipelines to ensure observability throughout your software lifecycle. You can:

- View deployment impact using release annotations

- Automate rollbacks if key performance metrics degrade

- Monitor infrastructure as code deployments

Example of setting a deployment marker in a pipeline:

```
az monitor app-insights events track --app <APP_NAME> --name
"Deployment" --properties "Version=1.2.3"
```

This helps correlate deployments with anomalies and assess rollout success.

Cost Considerations

Both Azure Monitor and Application Insights are metered based on data ingestion and retention. To manage cost:

- Enable **sampling** (fixed or adaptive)

- Limit retention periods

- Archive long-term logs to **Azure Storage**

- Regularly review data volume in Usage and Estimated Costs

Cost optimization does not mean reducing observability—it's about being intentional with your telemetry.

Summary

Using Azure Monitor and Application Insights is essential for modern cloud application development. These tools provide powerful observability capabilities across your application stack, enabling faster debugging, performance optimization, and reliability assurance.

By integrating monitoring into every stage of your development lifecycle, from code to production, you ensure that your applications remain responsive, resilient, and secure in the dynamic cloud environment.

Understanding Azure Security Center

Azure Security Center (ASC) is a unified infrastructure security management system that strengthens the security posture of your data centers and provides advanced threat protection across all your Azure and hybrid workloads. It delivers continuous assessment, actionable recommendations, and intelligent threat detection to help safeguard your cloud resources from evolving cyber threats.

Security is a shared responsibility between the cloud provider and the customer. With Azure Security Center, Microsoft provides a centralized view of your security state, enabling you to take necessary actions across all your subscriptions, resources, and environments.

Key Features of Azure Security Center

Azure Security Center offers a wide array of security capabilities designed to keep your cloud and hybrid environments protected:

- **Security Posture Management**: Continuous assessment of your Azure environment's security configurations and posture against best practices and regulatory compliance.

- **Secure Score**: A numerical summary that reflects the current state of your security configuration and recommendations to improve it.

- **Threat Protection**: Real-time threat detection across virtual machines, containers, databases, and other services.

- **Just-In-Time VM Access**: Minimizes exposure to brute-force attacks by controlling time-bound access to virtual machines.

- **File Integrity Monitoring**: Detects unauthorized changes to files and registry keys.

- **Adaptive Application Controls**: Controls which applications can run on your VMs, preventing malware execution.

- **Regulatory Compliance**: Maps your configuration against regulatory standards like ISO 27001, SOC TSP, NIST, and more.

Security Posture Management

Security posture management is the proactive approach ASC takes to continuously evaluate your resources for vulnerabilities, misconfigurations, and potential improvements.

The **Secure Score** helps you understand and quantify your security health. It evaluates the security of your Azure resources and provides improvement recommendations. Each recommendation has an associated impact on your secure score and, when resolved, helps reduce overall risk.

You can view and act on your Secure Score by:

1. Navigating to **Microsoft Defender for Cloud** in the Azure Portal.

2. Viewing the dashboard to see the current Secure Score.

3. Clicking on the score to drill down into the specific issues and recommendations.

Improving your Secure Score should be a regular activity and part of your DevSecOps process.

Enabling Azure Security Center

Azure Security Center is enabled by default at the Free tier for all Azure subscriptions. To access advanced features like threat protection and just-in-time VM access, you'll need to enable the **Standard** tier.

To enable Security Center:

1. Go to the **Azure Portal**.

2. Search for **Microsoft Defender for Cloud**.

3. Select your subscription.

4. Click **Environment Settings**, choose the subscription or management group, and select **Upgrade** to the Standard tier.

You can also automate this process using the Azure CLI:

```
az security pricing create --name VirtualMachines --tier 'Standard'
```

Repeat this for all relevant resource types to ensure full protection coverage.

Just-In-Time VM Access

Virtual machines with open ports are often the target of brute-force attacks. Just-In-Time (JIT) access reduces this risk by limiting access to specific ports for a limited duration and only from approved IP addresses.

To configure JIT access:

1. Go to **Microsoft Defender for Cloud > Inventory**.

2. Select a VM and choose **Just-In-Time VM access**.

3. Enable JIT, define the ports (e.g., SSH 22, RDP 3389), allowed IP ranges, and max duration.

Requests for access must be approved and are logged for auditing.

Programmatic configuration using Azure CLI:

```
az security jit-policy create --location eastus --resource-group
MyResourceGroup --name MyVM \
--jit-policy '[
  {
    "id":
"/subscriptions/<subscriptionId>/resourceGroups/MyResourceGroup/prov
iders/Microsoft.Compute/virtualMachines/MyVM",
    "ports": [
      {
        "number": 22,
        "protocol": "*",
        "allowedSourceAddressPrefix": "*",
        "maxRequestAccessDuration": "PT1H"
      }
```

```
        ]
    }
] '
```

JIT helps enforce least-privilege access and reduces exposure time windows.

Adaptive Application Controls

Azure Security Center can analyze your virtual machines and suggest application whitelisting rules. This feature ensures only approved applications can run, significantly reducing the risk of malicious software execution.

To enable application controls:

1. Go to **Defender for Cloud** > **Workload Protections** > **Adaptive Application Controls**.

2. Select a VM group, review the recommended allowed apps.

3. Enable control to block unknown applications.

This approach is especially useful in production environments where change should be tightly controlled.

Threat Detection

Security Center leverages Microsoft Threat Intelligence to detect real-world attacks such as:

- Brute-force login attempts

- Remote code execution

- Malware infections

- Suspicious PowerShell activity

- Lateral movement and persistence tactics

Detected threats appear under the **Security Alerts** section. Each alert includes:

- A description of the threat

- Affected resources

- Remediation guidance

- A severity level

You can configure alert rules to automatically notify teams or integrate with SIEM tools like Microsoft Sentinel, Splunk, or IBM QRadar.

Alerts can also trigger automated responses with Azure Logic Apps. For example, isolate a VM or disable a compromised user account.

Regulatory Compliance and Standards

Security Center includes **Regulatory Compliance Dashboard**, which helps assess your resource configuration against industry standards like:

- ISO 27001

- NIST SP 800-53

- Azure CIS Benchmark

- PCI DSS

- SOC TSP

Each control is evaluated continuously, and recommendations are provided for non-compliant resources. This makes it easier for organizations to align their infrastructure with required regulations and simplify audits.

You can add additional standards to your compliance dashboard:

1. Go to **Regulatory Compliance** in Microsoft Defender for Cloud.

2. Click **Manage Compliance Policies**.

3. Add the required standard.

All results are exportable and can be integrated into external compliance management systems.

Security Recommendations and Quick Fixes

Security Center surfaces actionable recommendations categorized by:

- Compute & apps

- Data & storage

- Networking

- Identity & access

- Security best practices

Each recommendation includes:

- Impact on Secure Score

- Description and remediation steps

- Option to apply a "quick fix" directly from the portal

For example, if a storage account is missing encryption, you'll be prompted to enable it and can do so in one click.

You can automate recommendations with Azure Policy. Use built-in policies or create custom ones that enforce specific configurations such as:

```
{
  "if": {
    "field": "type",
    "equals": "Microsoft.Storage/storageAccounts"
  },
  "then": {
    "effect": "deny",
    "details": {
      "type": "Microsoft.Security/policies",
      "name": "RequireEncryptionAtRest"
    }
  }
}
```

Deploy policies via ARM templates, Bicep, or Terraform to ensure infrastructure remains compliant over time.

Integration with Microsoft Defender and Other Services

Azure Security Center integrates tightly with other Microsoft Defender products for comprehensive protection:

- **Microsoft Defender for Endpoint**: Protects client endpoints with EDR (Endpoint Detection and Response).

- **Microsoft Defender for Identity**: Monitors Active Directory for identity-based attacks.

- **Microsoft Defender for SQL**: Monitors SQL servers for vulnerabilities and suspicious activity.

These integrations form a multi-layered defense system that correlates signals across the stack, from endpoints to databases to users.

Monitoring Security Center with Azure Monitor

All security alerts and recommendations can be piped into Azure Monitor for deeper analysis and correlation.

For example, use Log Analytics to query security alerts:

```
SecurityAlert
| where TimeGenerated > ago(1d)
| summarize count() by AlertName, Severity
```

You can create alerts and dashboards based on this data, integrating it with broader observability efforts.

Additionally, connect ASC to **Microsoft Sentinel** for advanced threat hunting using notebooks, playbooks, and incident response orchestration.

Summary

Azure Security Center is a powerful, centralized platform that provides advanced threat protection and continuous security posture management for your Azure and hybrid environments. From enforcing best practices to detecting live threats, ASC equips developers and operations teams with tools to build, deploy, and manage secure applications.

Leveraging Azure Security Center is a must for any organization that takes cloud security seriously. Its automation, integration, and intelligence help reduce the complexity of securing diverse environments, enabling proactive and resilient security strategies in today's fast-evolving threat landscape.

Setting Alerts and Diagnostics

Effective cloud application management requires proactive strategies to identify and respond to potential issues before they impact users. Azure provides robust tools for **alerts and**

diagnostics, enabling developers and operations teams to track metrics, analyze logs, detect anomalies, and take automated action when thresholds are breached.

Azure's alerting and diagnostics systems are part of **Azure Monitor** and integrate seamlessly with **Application Insights, Azure Security Center**, and **Log Analytics**. These features help maintain application health, ensure compliance, and support business continuity by providing deep insights into system behavior.

Types of Alerts in Azure

Azure supports multiple types of alerts, each tailored for specific use cases:

- **Metric Alerts**: Triggered based on time-series data such as CPU usage, request count, or memory consumption.

- **Log Alerts**: Generated from custom queries using Kusto Query Language (KQL) over log data.

- **Activity Log Alerts**: Based on events from the Azure Activity Log, useful for monitoring administrative operations.

- **Prometheus Alerts**: Used with Azure Monitor for containers, leveraging PromQL queries.

- **Smart Alerts (Dynamic Thresholds)**: Automatically detect anomalies and suggest thresholds based on historical data patterns.

Each alert can be configured with an **action group**, which defines the notification method and automation to invoke when the alert fires.

Creating Metric Alerts

Metric alerts monitor numeric performance indicators. Here's how to set one for CPU usage:

1. Navigate to **Azure Monitor** in the Azure Portal.

2. Click on **Alerts > + New alert rule**.

3. Select the target resource (e.g., a virtual machine or App Service).

4. Under **Condition**, choose the metric (e.g., `Percentage CPU`) and define the threshold (e.g., greater than 80% for 5 minutes).

5. Add an **action group** for notifications (email, SMS, webhook, Logic App, etc.).

6. Name the alert and create it.

CLI example:

```
az monitor metrics alert create \
  --name HighCPUAlert \
  --resource-group MyResourceGroup \
  --scopes /subscriptions/<subscription-
id>/resourceGroups/MyResourceGroup/providers/Microsoft.Compute/virtu
alMachines/MyVM \
  --condition "avg Percentage CPU > 80" \
  --description "Alert when CPU usage is over 80%"
```

This approach ensures timely detection of performance degradation.

Creating Log Alerts

Log alerts use queries written in KQL to analyze logs and identify conditions of interest. For example, to detect multiple failed login attempts:

```
SigninLogs
| where ResultType != 0
| summarize FailedLogins = count() by bin(TimeGenerated, 5m)
| where FailedLogins > 10
```

To create a log alert:

1. Go to **Log Analytics Workspace**.

2. Run your query to verify results.

3. Click **New Alert Rule** in the query results window.

4. Set the frequency and threshold.

5. Attach an action group.

Log alerts are ideal for security use cases, anomalies, and application-level issues.

Action Groups

Action groups are reusable configurations that define what happens when an alert fires. You can include:

- **Email** notifications

- **SMS** messages

- **Push** notifications

- **Voice** calls

- **Webhook** calls

- **Automation Runbooks**

- **Azure Functions**

- **Logic Apps**

- **ITSM connectors** (e.g., ServiceNow)

Example CLI to create an action group:

```
az monitor action-group create \
  --name NotifyTeam \
  --resource-group MyResourceGroup \
  --short-name Notify \
  --email-receiver name=DevOpsTeam email=devops@example.com
```

Once created, this group can be associated with any alert rule.

Configuring Diagnostic Settings

Diagnostic settings determine which telemetry data is collected and where it is sent. You can route logs and metrics to:

- Log Analytics

- Event Hubs

- Azure Storage accounts

To configure diagnostics:

1. Go to the resource (e.g., Key Vault, App Service).

2. Click on **Diagnostics settings**.

3. Add a new setting, name it, and select categories (e.g., `AuditLogs`, `PerformanceCounters`).

4. Choose the destination (e.g., Log Analytics Workspace).

This enables long-term retention, deeper analysis, and integration with third-party SIEMs.

Example using Azure CLI:

```
az monitor diagnostic-settings create \
  --name SendDiagnostics \
  --resource /subscriptions/<sub-
id>/resourceGroups/MyGroup/providers/Microsoft.Web/sites/MyApp \
  --workspace /subscriptions/<sub-
id>/resourceGroups/MyGroup/providers/Microsoft.OperationalInsights/w
orkspaces/MyWorkspace \
  --logs '[{"category": "AppServiceHTTPLogs", "enabled": true}]'
```

Diagnostic logs are crucial for incident forensics, usage analytics, and security investigations.

Advanced Alerting with Dynamic Thresholds

Dynamic Thresholds use machine learning to detect anomalies in metric patterns without needing to define fixed thresholds manually. Azure Monitor analyzes historical data to determine what constitutes abnormal behavior.

When creating a metric alert:

- Choose a metric (e.g., request count).

- Select **Dynamic** as the threshold type.

- Let Azure analyze historical data to create intelligent bounds.

Dynamic thresholds reduce noise from static rules and help catch early indicators of issues that fixed thresholds might miss.

Autoscaling Based on Alerts

Alerts can trigger autoscaling actions via integration with Azure Virtual Machine Scale Sets or App Service Plans.

To configure autoscaling:

1. Go to the target resource.

2. Select **Scaling**.

3. Define rules (e.g., add an instance if CPU > 75% for 10 minutes).

4. Optionally, link alerts to inform teams when scaling events occur.

This ensures elasticity and performance while maintaining operational transparency.

Alert Rules Best Practices

To get the most from Azure Alerts:

- **Group by severity**: Use severity levels (0 = Critical to 4 = Informational) to triage alerts.

- **Deduplicate**: Avoid multiple alerts for the same issue using smart thresholds and suppression rules.

- **Include context**: Customize alert messages with diagnostic context and resource metadata.

- **Use tags**: Filter alerts by environment (e.g., production vs. staging) using resource tags.

- **Integrate with DevOps tools**: Forward alerts to Slack, Teams, Jira, or other collaboration platforms.

Automating Responses with Logic Apps

Alerts can trigger Logic Apps to automate common responses like restarting services, notifying teams, or isolating compromised resources.

Example scenario: Restart an App Service when a high error rate is detected.

1. Create a Logic App with an HTTP trigger.

2. Define actions such as calling Azure REST API to restart the service.

3. Attach this Logic App to an alert action group.

This turns your alerting pipeline into an automated incident management system.

Monitoring Alert Activity

You can view alert history and performance in the **Alerts** pane of Azure Monitor. This includes:

- Active and resolved alerts

- Alert rule state

- Fired counts and trends

Use KQL to analyze alert frequency:

```
AlertRule
| summarize FiredCount = count() by RuleName, Severity
```

This helps you identify noisy rules and optimize alert configurations.

Exporting Alert Data

Alert and diagnostic data can be exported for:

- Compliance reports

- Audit logs

- External analytics

You can export alert history to CSV from the portal or use the REST API:

```
az monitor alert list --resource-group MyResourceGroup --output
table
```

Additionally, connect diagnostic logs to Event Hubs for streaming to third-party systems like Splunk, Datadog, or Elastic Stack.

Cost Management for Alerts and Diagnostics

Azure charges for certain monitoring features:

- Metric alerts: Free up to a quota

- Log alerts: Based on data scanned

- Diagnostic data: Based on storage and ingestion volume

To control costs:

- **Use sampling** in Application Insights.

- **Adjust retention policies** in Log Analytics.

- **Route infrequent logs to Blob Storage** instead of Log Analytics.

- **Review usage metrics** in Azure Cost Management.

By optimizing what you monitor and how you store it, you can maintain observability without exceeding your budget.

Summary

Alerts and diagnostics are foundational components of any well-architected cloud application. Azure offers a comprehensive, flexible system that allows teams to observe behavior, detect anomalies, respond rapidly to incidents, and automate remediations.

By thoughtfully configuring metric and log alerts, leveraging diagnostic settings, and using action groups for automation, teams can stay informed and in control. When used effectively, these tools transform monitoring from a reactive process into a strategic enabler of reliability, performance, and user satisfaction.

Compliance and Identity Management

Ensuring compliance with industry standards and maintaining secure identity management are core pillars of building robust applications in the cloud. Azure provides a comprehensive suite of tools that help developers and administrators manage compliance requirements, enforce identity policies, and control access with granular precision.

As regulations around data privacy, user consent, and governance continue to grow (e.g., GDPR, HIPAA, ISO 27001, NIST), organizations are increasingly relying on cloud-native compliance and identity management frameworks. Azure meets these needs with integrated solutions that address everything from user authentication to role-based access control and audit logging.

Understanding Azure Compliance Framework

Azure has a deeply integrated **compliance framework** that aligns with over 100 global standards and regulations. These include:

- **General Data Protection Regulation (GDPR)**

- **Health Insurance Portability and Accountability Act (HIPAA)**

- **ISO/IEC 27001**

- **National Institute of Standards and Technology (NIST)**

- **Service Organization Control (SOC 1, 2, and 3)**

- **Federal Risk and Authorization Management Program (FedRAMP)**

You can access Azure's compliance documentation and certifications from the Microsoft Trust Center.

In Azure, compliance is not just a checkbox but a set of enforceable configurations, best practices, and ongoing monitoring systems.

Azure enables compliance through:

- Built-in **Azure Policy** definitions

- **Blueprints** for regulated workloads

- **Regulatory Compliance Dashboards** in Microsoft Defender for Cloud

- **Audit logs** and **activity tracking**

Regulatory Compliance Dashboard

The **Regulatory Compliance Dashboard**, found in **Microsoft Defender for Cloud**, provides a consolidated view of how your Azure resources align with selected compliance standards. It continuously evaluates your environment and lists control failures, passing controls, and recommendations.

To access:

1. Open **Microsoft Defender for Cloud**.

2. Select **Regulatory Compliance**.

3. Choose a standard (e.g., NIST 800-53 or ISO 27001).

4. Review assessments grouped by control family (e.g., Access Control, Logging, Encryption).

5. Implement recommended remediations.

You can also create custom initiatives or compliance standards using Azure Policy. For example, if you need to enforce a specific regional law or internal governance requirement.

```
{
  "if": {
    "field": "location",
    "notEquals": "UK South"
  },
  "then": {
    "effect": "deny"
  }
}
```

This policy restricts resource deployment to UK South only—useful for data residency regulations.

Azure Policy and Blueprints

Azure Policy enables you to create, assign, and manage policies that enforce rules and effects over your resources. Azure evaluates resource properties and takes appropriate actions such as denying deployments or auditing compliance.

For example, you can enforce that all storage accounts must have encryption enabled:

```
{
  "if": {
    "allOf": [
      {
        "field": "type",
        "equals": "Microsoft.Storage/storageAccounts"
      },
      {
        "field":
"Microsoft.Storage/storageAccounts/supportsHttpsTrafficOnly",
        "equals": "false"
      }
    ]
  },
  "then": {
    "effect": "deny"
  }
}
```

Azure Blueprints allow you to package policies, RBAC roles, resource templates, and ARM definitions to set up governed environments rapidly. This is especially useful in regulated industries (e.g., finance, healthcare) where environments must meet specific criteria from day one.

You can assign blueprints at the subscription or management group level to maintain standardization across teams and projects.

Identity and Access Management (IAM) in Azure

Azure's Identity and Access Management system is built around **Azure Active Directory (Azure AD)**. Azure AD is a cloud-based identity provider that supports:

- User and group management

- Multi-factor authentication (MFA)

- Single Sign-On (SSO)

- Device identity

- Role-Based Access Control (RBAC)

- Conditional Access

You can secure applications and APIs, integrate with on-premises directories, and federate identities with external providers (e.g., Google, Facebook, GitHub).

Azure AD Users and Groups

Users and groups form the foundation of access control. Groups can be used to simplify permission assignment and policy targeting.

Creating a new user with CLI:

```
az ad user create --display-name "John Doe" --user-principal-name
john.doe@mydomain.com \
--password "ComplexP@ssword123" --force-change-password-next-login
true
```

Assigning a user to a group:

```
az ad group member add --group "Developers" --member-id <user-
object-id>
```

Azure AD groups can also be dynamic, automatically adding members based on user properties such as department or location.

Role-Based Access Control (RBAC)

RBAC allows fine-grained access management to Azure resources. Permissions are assigned to **principals** (users, groups, service principals, or managed identities) through **roles** at different **scopes** (subscription, resource group, or individual resources).

Built-in roles include:

- **Owner** – full access including role assignment

- **Contributor** – full access excluding role assignment

- **Reader** – view-only access

- **Storage Blob Data Reader** – access to blob data only

Assigning a contributor role at the resource group level:

```
az role assignment create \
  --assignee <user-object-id> \
  --role "Contributor" \
  --scope /subscriptions/<sub-id>/resourceGroups/MyResourceGroup
```

For least-privilege access, create **custom roles** defining only necessary permissions.

```
{
  "Name": "VM Monitor",
  "Actions": [
    "Microsoft.Compute/virtualMachines/read",
    "Microsoft.Insights/metrics/read"
  ],
  "AssignableScopes": [
    "/subscriptions/<sub-id>"
  ]
}
```

Multi-Factor Authentication (MFA)

MFA is one of the most effective ways to prevent unauthorized access. Azure AD supports MFA through:

- Microsoft Authenticator app

- Text messages

- Phone calls

- FIDO2 security keys

MFA can be enforced via Conditional Access policies.

Conditional Access

Conditional Access enforces policies based on signals such as:

- User/group

- Device compliance

- Location

- Application

- Risk detection

A common policy might require MFA only when users are outside a trusted IP range:

```
If:
  Location != Trusted_Network
Then:
  Require MFA
```

Policies are evaluated in real-time during sign-in and provide a critical layer of identity security.

Managed Identities for Azure Resources

Managed Identities simplify identity management for applications running on Azure. They allow your apps to authenticate to Azure services without storing credentials.

There are two types:

- **System-assigned**: Tied to a single resource, deleted when the resource is deleted.

- **User-assigned**: Standalone identities that can be shared across resources.

Example: Using a system-assigned identity to access Key Vault secrets from an App Service:

1. Enable managed identity in App Service.

2. Grant it access in Key Vault (Reader + Get permissions).

3. Use the Azure SDK to retrieve the secret securely.

```
var client = new SecretClient(new
Uri("https://myvault.vault.azure.net/"), new
DefaultAzureCredential());
var secret = await client.GetSecretAsync("MySecret");
```

This pattern eliminates hardcoded credentials and improves security posture.

Access Reviews and Audit Logs

Azure AD offers **Access Reviews** to ensure that users only have access they still require. This is useful for compliance and preventing privilege creep.

Configure reviews by:

1. Defining the scope (e.g., group or application).

2. Setting the reviewers (e.g., managers).

3. Scheduling the recurrence.

Audit Logs and **Sign-in Logs** provide visibility into identity operations:

- Who accessed what and when

- Password changes

- Group memberships

- Sign-in failures and suspicious behavior

You can access these logs via Azure Portal, download them as CSV, or query with KQL in Log Analytics:

```
AuditLogs
| where ActivityDisplayName == "Add member to group"
```

```
| project InitiatedBy, TargetResources, ActivityDateTime
```

Identity Governance and Lifecycle

Azure AD supports advanced identity governance capabilities:

- **Entitlement Management**: Bundle roles and apps into access packages for self-service.

- **Privileged Identity Management (PIM)**: Just-in-time access to high-privilege roles.

- **Identity Protection**: Risk-based policies that detect compromised accounts.

With **PIM**, admins can activate roles temporarily, require MFA, and generate approval workflows.

Example: Assigning PIM to a subscription Owner role with time-limited activation and audit logging ensures tighter security around critical resources.

Summary

Azure's compliance and identity management features provide a powerful, flexible framework to govern access, meet regulatory requirements, and secure your applications and data. By leveraging Azure Policy, Azure AD, RBAC, managed identities, and compliance dashboards, developers and IT administrators can implement a zero-trust security model and maintain compliance with industry standards.

Whether you're managing enterprise workloads or scaling SaaS products in regulated industries, these tools allow you to automate compliance, enforce consistent access controls, and provide security-by-design across your entire cloud footprint.

Chapter 8: Scaling and Performance Optimization

Auto-scaling Azure Services

Scalability is one of the core advantages of cloud computing, and Azure provides extensive capabilities to automatically scale resources in response to demand. Auto-scaling ensures that your application can handle changes in load without manual intervention, while also optimizing costs by scaling down during periods of low activity.

What is Auto-scaling?

Auto-scaling is the ability of a cloud platform to automatically adjust compute resources based on load, usage metrics, or schedules. Azure enables auto-scaling for a variety of services, including App Services, Virtual Machine Scale Sets, Azure Kubernetes Service (AKS), and Azure Functions.

With auto-scaling, you can configure rules to add or remove instances of a service or adjust resource allocation dynamically. This ensures high performance, availability, and cost efficiency.

Types of Scaling

There are two primary types of scaling:

- **Vertical Scaling (Scale Up/Down)**: Increasing or decreasing the capacity of an existing resource, such as upgrading a VM size.

- **Horizontal Scaling (Scale Out/In)**: Adding or removing instances of a resource, such as creating additional web server instances to handle increased traffic.

Azure supports both, but horizontal scaling is generally preferred for cloud-native applications due to its efficiency and fault tolerance.

Configuring Auto-scale in Azure App Service

Azure App Services offer a built-in auto-scaling mechanism based on rules and schedules. To configure auto-scaling:

1. Navigate to your App Service in the Azure Portal.

2. Select "Scale out (App Service Plan)" under the Settings section.

3. Click "+ Add a rule".

4. Define the condition (e.g., CPU Percentage > 70%).

5. Set the action (e.g., increase instance count by 1).

6. Set cooldown periods and instance limits to avoid rapid scaling.

Here's a sample auto-scale rule configuration in Azure Resource Manager (ARM) template:

```json
{
  "type": "Microsoft.Insights/autoscalesettings",
  "apiVersion": "2015-04-01",
  "name": "[concat(parameters('appServicePlanName'), '-
autoscale')]",
  "location": "[resourceGroup().location]",
  "properties": {
    "enabled": true,
    "targetResourceUri": "[resourceId('Microsoft.Web/serverfarms',
parameters('appServicePlanName'))]",
    "profiles": [
      {
        "name": "AutoScaleProfile",
        "capacity": {
          "minimum": "1",
          "maximum": "5",
          "default": "1"
        },
        "rules": [
          {
            "metricTrigger": {
              "metricName": "CpuPercentage",
              "metricNamespace": "",
              "metricResourceUri":
"[resourceId('Microsoft.Web/serverfarms',
parameters('appServicePlanName'))]",
              "timeGrain": "PT1M",
              "statistic": "Average",
              "timeWindow": "PT5M",
              "timeAggregation": "Average",
              "operator": "GreaterThan",
              "threshold": 70.0
            },
            "scaleAction": {
```

```json
        "direction": "Increase",
        "type": "ChangeCount",
        "value": "1",
        "cooldown": "PT5M"
      }
    }
  ]
}
]
}
}
```

Auto-scaling with Azure Virtual Machine Scale Sets

Azure Virtual Machine Scale Sets (VMSS) allow you to deploy and manage a set of identical, load-balanced VMs. VMSS integrates tightly with the Azure autoscale engine, supporting both custom metrics and predefined metrics like CPU usage.

To enable autoscale for VMSS:

1. Go to your VMSS in the Azure Portal.

2. Select "Scaling".

3. Set minimum, maximum, and default instance count.

4. Add scale-out and scale-in rules based on metrics like CPU or memory.

Here's an example of an Azure CLI command to set autoscale rules for a VMSS:

```
az monitor autoscale create \
  --resource-group MyResourceGroup \
  --resource /subscriptions/{subscription-
id}/resourceGroups/MyResourceGroup/providers/Microsoft.Compute/virtu
alMachineScaleSets/MyVMSS \
  --resource-type Microsoft.Compute/virtualMachineScaleSets \
  --name autoscale-vmss \
  --min-count 1 \
  --max-count 10 \
  --count 2

az monitor autoscale rule create \
  --resource-group MyResourceGroup \
```

```
  --autoscale-name autoscale-vmss \
  --condition "Percentage CPU > 70 avg 5m" \
  --scale out 1

az monitor autoscale rule create \
  --resource-group MyResourceGroup \
  --autoscale-name autoscale-vmss \
  --condition "Percentage CPU < 30 avg 5m" \
  --scale in 1
```

Scaling Azure Kubernetes Service (AKS)

AKS supports two types of scaling:

- **Cluster Autoscaler**: Automatically adjusts the number of nodes in your cluster.

- **Horizontal Pod Autoscaler (HPA)**: Automatically scales the number of pods in a deployment based on CPU or memory usage.

To enable Cluster Autoscaler in AKS:

```
az aks update \
  --resource-group MyResourceGroup \
  --name MyAKSCluster \
  --enable-cluster-autoscaler \
  --min-count 1 \
  --max-count 5
```

To enable HPA:

```
kubectl autoscale deployment my-deployment \
  --cpu-percent=50 \
  --min=1 \
  --max=10
```

Auto-scaling Azure Functions

Azure Functions scale automatically based on the number of incoming events. The Consumption Plan handles this out-of-the-box, and you don't need to manually configure scaling. However, the Premium Plan and Dedicated Plans provide more control and predictable performance.

For time-sensitive or memory-intensive workloads, consider using the Premium Plan which supports VNET integration and scaling out more quickly.

Scheduled Scaling

Sometimes, traffic patterns are predictable (e.g., more traffic during business hours). In such cases, scheduled scaling is more efficient than reactive scaling.

Azure supports scheduled scaling as part of the autoscale configuration. You can specify different rules for different time windows.

Example:

- Increase to 5 instances every weekday at 9 AM.

- Decrease to 1 instance every weekday at 6 PM.

This can be configured through the Azure Portal or defined in your ARM templates or Bicep files.

Best Practices for Auto-scaling

- **Set proper thresholds**: Monitor performance and adjust threshold values to prevent over-scaling or under-scaling.

- **Include cooldown periods**: Prevent flapping by setting cooldown periods between scale actions.

- **Use metrics that reflect workload**: CPU may not always be the best indicator. Use custom metrics like queue length, request count, or memory usage where appropriate.

- **Test autoscale behavior**: Simulate load to ensure autoscale rules are correctly configured and respond as expected.

- **Implement logging and monitoring**: Use Azure Monitor and Application Insights to observe how scaling affects performance and cost.

Monitoring and Logging Auto-scale Events

Azure Monitor captures all autoscale events and allows you to set alerts or view trends over time. You can review scaling history, failures, and metrics to ensure scaling rules are behaving correctly.

To view autoscale events:

1. Navigate to Azure Monitor.

2. Select "Autoscale".

3. Choose your resource and review the activity log and metric charts.

You can also create alerts using Azure Monitor to notify administrators of scale actions:

```
az monitor metrics alert create \
  --name "scale-alert" \
  --resource-group MyResourceGroup \
  --scopes "/subscriptions/{subscription-
id}/resourceGroups/MyResourceGroup/providers/Microsoft.Web/sites/MyA
ppService" \
  --condition "avg CpuPercentage > 80" \
  --window-size 5m \
  --evaluation-frequency 1m \
  --action "/subscriptions/{subscription-
id}/resourceGroups/MyResourceGroup/providers/microsoft.insights/acti
onGroups/MyActionGroup"
```

Conclusion

Auto-scaling is a critical feature for modern cloud-native applications. Azure provides a robust and flexible set of tools to scale compute resources, services, and containers dynamically. Whether you're running simple web apps or complex microservices, leveraging autoscaling ensures your applications remain responsive, resilient, and cost-effective.

To implement effective autoscaling:

- Use the right type of scaling (vertical or horizontal) for your application.

- Configure smart rules based on accurate metrics.

- Monitor usage and adjust parameters as needed.

- Test your autoscale setup to confirm expected behavior.

As workloads and user expectations evolve, having a dynamic scaling strategy is not just a luxury—it's a necessity for sustainable application growth in the cloud.

Load Balancers and Traffic Managers

Building resilient and performant cloud applications requires careful planning for load distribution and failover handling. Azure provides several services that support efficient routing and load balancing of traffic across resources, ensuring both high availability and optimal performance. This section will explore Azure Load Balancer and Azure Traffic Manager in depth, along with scenarios, configurations, and best practices.

Understanding Load Balancing in Azure

Load balancing is the process of distributing incoming network traffic across multiple backend resources, such as virtual machines or app instances. This ensures that no single resource is overwhelmed and improves overall application reliability and performance.

Azure provides multiple load balancing solutions:

- **Azure Load Balancer**: Operates at layer 4 (TCP/UDP), offering high-performance, low-latency distribution.

- **Azure Application Gateway**: Operates at layer 7 (HTTP/HTTPS) and supports features like URL-based routing and SSL termination.

- **Azure Traffic Manager**: DNS-based traffic distribution across global endpoints for redundancy and performance optimization.

- **Azure Front Door**: Global HTTP/HTTPS load balancing with intelligent routing and acceleration.

Each service caters to specific needs and may be used in combination for hybrid or highly resilient architectures.

Azure Load Balancer

Azure Load Balancer distributes network traffic across backend resources within a region. It supports inbound and outbound scenarios for both internal and internet-facing applications.

Key Features:

- Layer 4 (TCP/UDP) load balancing

- High availability and performance

- Health probes for endpoint monitoring

- Support for inbound NAT rules

Types of Azure Load Balancer:

1. **Basic Load Balancer**: Suitable for dev/test environments.

2. **Standard Load Balancer**: Recommended for production workloads. Offers better performance, diagnostics, and scalability.

Common Scenarios:

- Distributing requests across a VM scale set

- Supporting highly available multi-tier architectures

- Routing traffic to internal services in a VNET

Example: Creating a Standard Load Balancer via Azure CLI

```
az network lb create \
  --resource-group MyResourceGroup \
  --name MyLoadBalancer \
  --sku Standard \
  --frontend-ip-name MyFrontEndPool \
  --backend-pool-name MyBackEndPool \
  --location eastus
```

Add a health probe:

```
az network lb probe create \
  --resource-group MyResourceGroup \
  --lb-name MyLoadBalancer \
  --name MyHealthProbe \
  --protocol tcp \
  --port 80
```

Add a load-balancing rule:

```
az network lb rule create \
  --resource-group MyResourceGroup \
  --lb-name MyLoadBalancer \
  --name MyHTTPRule \
  --protocol tcp \
  --frontend-port 80 \
  --backend-port 80 \
  --frontend-ip-name MyFrontEndPool \
```

```
--backend-pool-name MyBackEndPool \
--probe-name MyHealthProbe
```

Azure Application Gateway

Application Gateway is a web traffic load balancer that enables you to manage traffic to web applications.

Features:

- URL-based routing

- SSL termination

- Web Application Firewall (WAF)

- Session affinity (cookie-based)

Use Cases:

- Routing traffic to different microservices based on URL path

- Protecting applications with a WAF

- Load balancing multiple web app instances

Sample Configuration for URL-Based Routing

If you have two applications `/api` and `/web`, you can configure Application Gateway rules like:

- Route `/api/*` to API backend pool

- Route `/web/*` to Web frontend pool

This can be configured via Azure Portal or ARM templates.

Azure Traffic Manager

Azure Traffic Manager is a DNS-based global traffic distribution service. It directs client requests to the most appropriate endpoint based on the configured routing method.

Key Routing Methods:

- **Priority**: Route to primary endpoint, failover to secondary.

- **Weighted**: Distribute based on weights (e.g., 70%-30%).

- **Performance**: Route to the closest endpoint (lowest latency).

- **Geographic**: Route based on geographic location of the user.

- **Multivalue**: Return multiple healthy endpoints.

- **Subnet**: Custom routing by IP range.

Use Cases:

- High availability with geographic redundancy

- Multi-region active-active setups

- Directing specific users to local datacenters

Example: Create Traffic Manager Profile (CLI)

```
az network traffic-manager profile create \
  --name myTrafficManager \
  --resource-group MyResourceGroup \
  --routing-method Performance \
  --unique-dns-name myapp-tm-profile \
  --ttl 30 \
  --protocol HTTP \
  --port 80 \
  --path "/"
```

Add endpoints:

```
az network traffic-manager endpoint create \
  --resource-group MyResourceGroup \
  --profile-name myTrafficManager \
  --name appEndpoint1 \
  --type azureEndpoints \
  --target-resource-id
"/subscriptions/xxx/resourceGroups/xxx/providers/Microsoft.Network/p
ublicIPAddresses/app-ip-1" \
  --endpoint-status Enabled
```

```
az network traffic-manager endpoint create \
  --resource-group MyResourceGroup \
  --profile-name myTrafficManager \
  --name appEndpoint2 \
  --type azureEndpoints \
  --target-resource-id
"/subscriptions/xxx/resourceGroups/xxx/providers/Microsoft.Network/p
ublicIPAddresses/app-ip-2" \
  --endpoint-status Enabled
```

Azure Front Door

Azure Front Door is a global, scalable entry point for web applications. It provides fast content delivery, SSL offloading, WAF, and intelligent load balancing across regions.

Features:

- Global HTTP/HTTPS load balancing

- Application acceleration (Anycast, caching)

- SSL certificate management

- WAF policies

- URL-based routing with rewrite rules

Use Case Example:

A multinational e-commerce platform routes traffic through Front Door to backend apps deployed in Europe, North America, and Asia. Users are automatically directed to the nearest backend for fastest performance and availability.

Front Door also supports failover in case of a region failure, with minimal disruption to users.

Choosing the Right Load Balancer

Requirement	Recommended Service
Low-level TCP/UDP load balancing	Azure Load Balancer
HTTP/HTTPS traffic with URL routing	Azure Application Gateway

Global traffic routing	Azure Traffic Manager
Global web acceleration and WAF	Azure Front Door

It's common to use these services in combination. For example:

- Azure Load Balancer + VMSS for internal backend scaling

- Application Gateway for frontend routing with WAF

- Traffic Manager for multi-region failover

- Front Door for performance and global web entry point

Monitoring Load Balancers and Traffic Routing

Monitoring is crucial to ensure that load balancing configurations are working effectively.

Azure Monitor, Application Insights, and Network Watcher provide diagnostics, metrics, and logs for:

- Request counts and response times

- Backend health and probe statuses

- Geographic routing performance

- Latency and error rates

You can configure alerts based on custom metrics (e.g., backend probe failure rate exceeding 10% over 5 minutes).

Example: Creating an alert rule on backend pool health:

```
az monitor metrics alert create \
  --name "BackendHealthAlert" \
  --resource-group MyResourceGroup \
  --scopes
"/subscriptions/xxx/resourceGroups/MyResourceGroup/providers/Microso
ft.Network/loadBalancers/MyLoadBalancer" \
  --condition "avg DipAvailability < 90" \
  --window-size 5m \
  --evaluation-frequency 1m \
```

```
  --action
"/subscriptions/xxx/resourceGroups/MyResourceGroup/providers/microso
ft.insights/actionGroups/MyActionGroup"
```

Best Practices

- **Health Probes**: Use reliable and specific health probes to detect endpoint issues.

- **Graceful Failover**: Implement traffic redirection in stages to prevent abrupt service loss.

- **Performance Testing**: Use tools like Azure Load Testing or JMeter to simulate traffic patterns.

- **Geo-Replication**: For global services, deploy to multiple regions and use Traffic Manager or Front Door for resilience.

- **Security**: Use WAF with Application Gateway or Front Door to protect against threats.

- **Observability**: Centralize metrics and logging for faster diagnostics and proactive issue resolution.

Conclusion

Azure offers a robust set of services for managing traffic distribution across your applications. Proper use of load balancers and traffic managers not only improves reliability but also ensures users receive the best experience regardless of their location or your infrastructure load.

By combining tools like Azure Load Balancer, Application Gateway, Traffic Manager, and Front Door, developers and architects can build highly available, scalable, and secure applications. These services support everything from basic VM scaling to global multi-region web platforms, making them essential components of modern cloud architectures.

Best Practices for High Availability

Ensuring high availability (HA) in cloud applications is critical for delivering reliable user experiences and minimizing downtime. In Azure, high availability encompasses strategies, configurations, and architectural decisions that allow services to remain operational under a variety of failure conditions, whether due to hardware faults, software bugs, network issues, or even entire region failures.

This section provides a comprehensive guide to implementing high availability in Azure applications, focusing on design principles, services, configurations, and real-world implementation strategies.

Understanding High Availability

High availability is the ability of an application or service to remain accessible and functional over time, even in the face of unexpected disruptions. In Azure, availability is often expressed in SLAs (Service Level Agreements), such as 99.9%, 99.99%, or 99.999% uptime.

For context:

- **99.9% uptime** = ~43 minutes of downtime/month

- **99.99% uptime** = ~4.3 minutes/month

- **99.999% uptime** = ~26 seconds/month

The goal is to design systems that minimize single points of failure (SPOFs), support fault tolerance, and recover gracefully from errors.

General Principles of High Availability

1. **Redundancy**: Duplicate critical components so that if one fails, others can take over.

2. **Failover**: Automate switching to standby systems when failures occur.

3. **Load Balancing**: Distribute traffic to avoid overloading any single resource.

4. **Health Monitoring**: Continuously check the status of resources and services.

5. **Geographic Distribution**: Deploy across multiple regions to handle region-specific failures.

6. **Statelessness**: Design services so that they do not rely on in-memory or local data to operate.

Azure Availability Zones and Regions

Azure offers a high-availability infrastructure using *Availability Zones* and *Regions*:

- **Availability Zones** are physically separate data centers within a region. Each zone has independent power, cooling, and networking. Deploying services across multiple zones protects against data center failures.

- **Regions** are geographically distinct locations. Cross-region redundancy helps protect against broader disasters or outages.

Many services in Azure support zone-redundant deployments, including:

- Azure App Service (Premium)

- Azure SQL Database (Business Critical)

- Azure Kubernetes Service (AKS)

- Azure Load Balancer and Application Gateway

Sample: Deploying a VM across Availability Zones (ARM snippet)

```
{
  "type": "Microsoft.Compute/virtualMachines",
  "apiVersion": "2021-07-01",
  "name": "myVM",
  "location": "[resourceGroup().location]",
  "zones": [ "1" ],
  "properties": {
    "hardwareProfile": {
      "vmSize": "Standard_DS1_v2"
    },
    ...
  }
}
```

To achieve HA, deploy multiple VMs in different zones and place them behind a load balancer.

High Availability for Azure App Services

Azure App Services support high availability by:

- Running multiple instances in a scale-out model

- Deploying in zone-redundant configurations (Premium plans)

- Utilizing Traffic Manager or Front Door for geo-distribution

Best Practices:

- Always run at least two instances.

- Enable autoscaling based on performance metrics.

- Use staging slots for zero-downtime deployments.

- Use Application Insights to monitor uptime and response times.

Database High Availability

Data persistence is often the most critical component for high availability. Azure provides various options:

Azure SQL Database

- Supports active geo-replication for cross-region disaster recovery.

- Zone-redundant configurations in the Business Critical tier.

- Automatic failover groups.

```
az sql failover-group create \
  --name MyFailoverGroup \
  --partner-server mysecondaryserver \
  --resource-group MyResourceGroup \
  --server myprimaryserver \
  --failover-policy Automatic \
  --grace-period 1
```

Cosmos DB

- Offers turnkey global distribution and multi-master support.

- Automatic failover and five 9s availability SLA.

- Configurable consistency levels (Strong, Bounded Staleness, Session, etc.)

```
az cosmosdb update \
  --name mycosmosdbaccount \
  --resource-group MyResourceGroup \
  --locations regionName=eastus failoverPriority=0 \
  --locations regionName=westeurope failoverPriority=1
```

Virtual Machines and VM Scale Sets

For applications that require full control of the infrastructure:

- Use **Availability Sets** for fault domain and update domain separation.

- Use **VM Scale Sets (VMSS)** for auto-scaling and distributing VMs across zones.

VMSS combined with Azure Load Balancer ensures both availability and scalability.

```
az vmss create \
  --resource-group MyResourceGroup \
  --name MyScaleSet \
  --image UbuntuLTS \
  --upgrade-policy-mode automatic \
  --admin-username azureuser \
  --generate-ssh-keys \
  --zones 1 2 3
```

Azure Kubernetes Service (AKS)

AKS offers built-in support for high availability:

- **Multi-node pools**: Distribute workloads across pools.

- **Availability zones**: Zone-aware scheduling.

- **Cluster Autoscaler**: Maintain optimal node count.

- **Pod Disruption Budgets**: Ensure that minimum pods are always available.

To create a zonal AKS cluster:

```
az aks create \
  --resource-group MyResourceGroup \
  --name MyAKSCluster \
  --node-count 3 \
  --zones 1 2 3 \
  --enable-cluster-autoscaler \
  --min-count 3 \
  --max-count 10
```

Use `livenessProbe` and `readinessProbe` in pod specs to ensure high availability at the application level.

Networking and DNS Redundancy

Combine **Azure Load Balancer**, **Application Gateway**, and **Azure Traffic Manager** or **Front Door** to route traffic intelligently.

- Use **internal load balancers** for backend services.

- Use **Application Gateway with WAF** for web apps.

- Use **Traffic Manager** for DNS-based region failover.

- Use **Azure DNS** with multiple name servers and alias records for failover.

Backup and Disaster Recovery

High availability is often confused with disaster recovery (DR). HA keeps your service running during small or medium failures. DR is about recovering from catastrophic events.

Azure offers native tools for DR:

- **Azure Site Recovery (ASR)**: Replicate VMs and workloads to another region.

- **Azure Backup**: Automated backups for VMs, databases, and files.

Example: Configuring ASR for VM replication

```
az backup vault create \
  --resource-group MyResourceGroup \
  --name MyRecoveryVault \
  --location eastus

az backup protection enable-for-vm \
  --resource-group MyResourceGroup \
  --vault-name MyRecoveryVault \
  --vm MyVM \
  --policy-name DefaultPolicy
```

CI/CD for High Availability

Deployment processes can introduce downtime if not handled correctly. Use CI/CD best practices to maintain HA:

- **Blue/Green Deployment**: Deploy to a new environment, switch traffic post-validation.

- **Canary Releases**: Gradually expose changes to a subset of users.

- **Rolling Updates**: Update services incrementally to reduce blast radius.

- **Staging Slots**: Use App Service deployment slots for safe swaps.

Monitoring and Alerting

Observability is essential to detect and respond to availability issues.

Use the following tools:

- **Azure Monitor**: Metrics and alerts

- **Application Insights**: Telemetry and tracing

- **Log Analytics**: Centralized log query

- **Service Health**: Platform issue notifications

Configure alerts:

```
az monitor metrics alert create \
  --name "CPUHigh" \
  --resource-group MyResourceGroup \
  --scopes
"/subscriptions/xxx/resourceGroups/xxx/providers/Microsoft.Compute/v
irtualMachines/MyVM" \
  --condition "avg Percentage CPU > 80" \
  --window-size 5m \
  --evaluation-frequency 1m \
  --action
"/subscriptions/xxx/resourceGroups/xxx/providers/microsoft.insights/
actionGroups/MyActionGroup"
```

Testing for High Availability

Even the best HA architecture must be validated. Perform the following:

- **Chaos Engineering**: Inject failures intentionally.

- **Simulated Region Failures**: Disconnect services to test DR response.

- **Load Testing**: Validate performance under high user loads.

- **Failover Drills**: Practice switching to standby systems.

Summary

High availability in Azure is not a single service or configuration but a mindset and a layered strategy. By combining geographic redundancy, resilient architectures, intelligent routing, and proactive monitoring, you can deliver robust and fault-tolerant cloud applications.

Key takeaways:

- Design for failure; assume components will break.

- Use availability zones and regions to distribute risk.

- Leverage native HA features of Azure services.

- Automate recovery and failover.

- Monitor continuously and respond proactively.

By adopting these practices, you can meet or exceed the demanding availability requirements of modern applications and ensure a seamless experience for your users across the globe.

Cost Management and Optimization

Managing and optimizing costs in cloud environments like Microsoft Azure is essential for ensuring long-term sustainability, maximizing return on investment, and maintaining fiscal responsibility. With the flexibility and scalability that Azure provides, it is easy for costs to spiral out of control if not carefully monitored and controlled. This section explores comprehensive strategies, tools, and best practices for effective cost management in Azure, including budgeting, monitoring, automation, and architectural decisions that contribute to cost efficiency.

The Pillars of Cost Optimization

Cost optimization in Azure can be categorized into five core areas:

1. **Visibility**: Understanding where and how money is being spent.

2. **Accountability**: Assigning ownership and responsibility for costs.

3. **Optimization**: Identifying opportunities to reduce costs.

4. **Automation**: Enforcing policies and making cost-saving actions automatic.

5. **Governance**: Defining controls to ensure sustainable cost practices.

Azure Cost Management and Billing Tools

Azure provides native tools for cost visibility and optimization:

- **Azure Cost Management + Billing**: A suite of tools to analyze, manage, and optimize your Azure spending.

- **Azure Advisor**: Personalized recommendations for cost optimization and performance.

- **Budgets and Alerts**: To track and control spending.

- **Pricing Calculator**: To estimate costs before provisioning resources.

- **TCO Calculator**: Compare on-premises vs Azure costs.

Azure Cost Management Portal

To access Azure Cost Management:

1. Navigate to the Azure Portal.

2. Select "Cost Management + Billing."

3. View cost analysis, trends, forecasts, and savings opportunities.

Creating a Budget

Creating a budget ensures you don't exceed planned spending.

```
az consumption budget create \
  --amount 1000 \
  --category cost \
  --name "MonthlyBudget" \
  --resource-group MyResourceGroup \
  --time-grain Monthly \
  --start-date 2025-01-01 \
  --end-date 2025-12-31 \
  --notifications \
```

```
    actualGreaterThan=90% \
    email=myemail@domain.com
```

This creates a budget of $1000 per month with alerts when 90% of the budget is used.

Resource Tagging for Cost Attribution

Tags are key-value pairs assigned to Azure resources. Proper tagging allows you to track spending by project, environment, department, or owner.

Example tags:

- `Environment=Production`

- `Department=Marketing`

- `Project=EcommercePlatform`

- `Owner=jane.doe@example.com`

Use tags to group costs in cost analysis views.

To apply a tag using CLI:

```
az tag create --resource-id
/subscriptions/{id}/resourceGroups/MyResourceGroup/providers/Microso
ft.Compute/virtualMachines/MyVM \
   --tags Department=IT Environment=Dev
```

You can enforce tagging using **Azure Policy** to ensure all resources are consistently tagged.

Rightsizing and Deallocation

Rightsizing involves adjusting resource sizes based on actual usage patterns. Many organizations overprovision for peak loads, resulting in wasted spend.

Common Examples:

- **VMs**: Scale down CPU/memory or switch to B-series (burstable) VMs.

- **App Services**: Move from Premium to Standard or from Standard to Basic during off-peak.

- **Storage**: Use cool or archive tiers for infrequently accessed data.

Azure Advisor provides recommendations for underutilized resources:

```
az advisor recommendation list --category Cost
```

Deallocate unused VMs during off-hours:

```
az vm deallocate --resource-group MyResourceGroup --name MyVM
```

Automate this with Azure Automation or Logic Apps based on a schedule.

Using Reserved Instances and Savings Plans

Azure offers **Reserved Instances (RIs)** and **Savings Plans** for predictable workloads.

- **RIs**: Commit to 1- or 3-year terms for compute resources (e.g., VMs, SQL).

- **Savings Plans**: Flexible pricing across VM sizes and regions with a committed hourly spend.

You can save up to 72% over pay-as-you-go rates.

To purchase a reserved instance:

1. Navigate to Azure Portal > Reservations.

2. Select the service (e.g., Virtual Machines).

3. Choose instance size, region, and term.

4. Review and purchase.

Use the **Reservation Utilization Report** to ensure you're making full use of your commitments.

Auto-scaling to Save Money

Auto-scaling isn't just about performance—it's also a key cost-saver. Ensure services like App Service, AKS, and VM Scale Sets automatically scale down during low usage periods.

Best Practices:

- Set conservative minimum instance counts.

- Use schedule-based scaling for predictable loads.

- Monitor usage and tweak rules over time.

Example: Schedule-based auto-scaling for App Service

```
{
  "location": "East US",
  "properties": {
    "profiles": [
      {
        "name": "Work Hours",
        "capacity": {
          "minimum": "2",
          "maximum": "5",
          "default": "2"
        },
        "recurrence": {
          "frequency": "Week",
          "schedule": {
            "timeZone": "UTC",
            "days": [ "Monday", "Tuesday", "Wednesday", "Thursday",
"Friday" ],
            "hours": [ 9 ],
            "minutes": [ 0 ]
          }
        }
      }
    ]
  }
}
```

Storage Optimization

Storage costs can escalate quickly. Azure offers various storage tiers to match cost with access frequency:

- **Hot**: Frequently accessed data.

- **Cool**: Infrequently accessed, lower cost.

- **Archive**: Rarely accessed, long-term storage.

Strategies:

- Move old blobs to archive tier using lifecycle management.

- Compress and deduplicate files.

- Use Azure Files Premium only for IOPS-intensive workloads.

Configure lifecycle rules:

```
az storage blob service-properties delete-policy update \
  --account-name mystorageaccount \
  --enable true \
  --days-retained 30
```

Cost-Aware Architectures

Architectural decisions have long-term cost implications.

Serverless

Use Azure Functions or Logic Apps for event-driven workloads. You only pay for execution time.

Containers

Use AKS or Azure Container Apps for microservices with bursty usage.

Multi-tenant Apps

Design SaaS platforms to share resources among tenants for better cost distribution.

Event-Driven Messaging

Use Azure Event Grid and Service Bus to decouple services and reduce compute overhead.

Governance and Policy Enforcement

Prevent cost overruns with built-in governance:

- **Azure Policy**: Restrict costly resource types (e.g., prevent creation of GPU VMs).

- **Management Groups**: Apply budgets and policies across departments or business units.

- **Role-Based Access Control (RBAC)**: Limit who can provision and manage resources.

Sample Policy: Prevent creation of unmanaged disks

```json
{
  "if": {
    "allOf": [
      {
        "field": "type",
        "equals": "Microsoft.Compute/disks"
      },
      {
        "field":
"Microsoft.Compute/disks.creationData.createOption",
        "equals": "Empty"
      }
    ]
  },
  "then": {
    "effect": "deny"
  }
}
```

Forecasting and Reporting

Azure Cost Management includes forecasting tools that use historical trends to predict future spending. Create scheduled reports to send cost summaries to stakeholders.

You can export cost data to Azure Storage or Power BI for advanced analysis:

```
az consumption usage list --start-date 2025-04-01 --end-date 2025-04-30
```

Third-Party Tools

In addition to Azure-native tools, consider these third-party solutions:

- **CloudHealth by VMware**

- **CloudCheckr**

- **Spot.io**

- **Apptio Cloudability**

These tools offer detailed analytics, anomaly detection, rightsizing recommendations, and multi-cloud cost governance.

Summary

Cost optimization in Azure is not a one-time activity—it's an ongoing practice that spans technical, operational, and organizational domains. By implementing the strategies in this section, you can dramatically reduce waste, improve efficiency, and align spending with business value.

Key Actions:

- Monitor continuously with Azure Cost Management.

- Tag resources for accountability.

- Use automation to enforce cost-saving actions.

- Right-size and deallocate idle resources.

- Apply reserved instances and savings plans.

- Architect with cost-awareness from the start.

Cloud cost optimization is as much about discipline as it is about tooling. Cultivate a culture of cost responsibility across teams, and use Azure's rich ecosystem of tools and services to stay ahead of your cloud budget.

Chapter 9: Real-World Project Scenarios

Building a Cloud-Native Web App

In this section, we'll walk through the development of a cloud-native web application using Microsoft Azure. A cloud-native approach means designing the application to fully leverage cloud services such as scalability, resiliency, and managed infrastructure, right from the beginning. Azure offers a wide array of services that allow developers to rapidly build and deploy powerful, scalable applications.

Project Overview

We'll build a task management web app called **CloudTasker**. It will allow users to create accounts, add tasks, mark them as completed, and organize them into categories. The application will use:

- **Azure App Services** for hosting the front-end and back-end

- **Azure SQL Database** for relational data storage

- **Azure Blob Storage** for optional file attachments

- **Azure Key Vault** for secure configuration management

- **Azure DevOps** for CI/CD

- **Azure Monitor and Application Insights** for diagnostics

Designing the Architecture

The architecture for our cloud-native app includes:

1. **Front-End**: React web app deployed to Azure App Service

2. **Back-End**: Node.js REST API deployed to Azure App Service

3. **Database**: Azure SQL Database

4. **Blob Storage**: To store file attachments

5. **Authentication**: Azure AD B2C

6. **Monitoring**: Azure Monitor, Application Insights

7. **Secrets Management**: Azure Key Vault

This separation allows for independent scaling, better fault isolation, and maintainability.

Step 1: Setting Up the Environment

1. Create a resource group

```
az group create --name CloudTaskerRG --location "East US"
```

2. Set up Azure SQL Database

```
az sql server create \
  --name cloudtaskersqlserver \
  --resource-group CloudTaskerRG \
  --location "East US" \
  --admin-user adminuser \
  --admin-password MyP@ssword123

az sql db create \
  --resource-group CloudTaskerRG \
  --server cloudtaskersqlserver \
  --name CloudTaskerDB \
  --service-objective S0
```

3. Configure firewall

```
az sql server firewall-rule create \
  --resource-group CloudTaskerRG \
  --server cloudtaskersqlserver \
  --name AllowYourIP \
  --start-ip-address YOUR_IP \
  --end-ip-address YOUR_IP
```

Step 2: Building the Back-End API

Technologies Used: Node.js, Express.js, Sequelize (ORM)

Database schema:

- Users

- Tasks

- Categories

```javascript
// models/task.js
module.exports = (sequelize, DataTypes) => {
  const Task = sequelize.define('Task', {
    title: DataTypes.STRING,
    completed: DataTypes.BOOLEAN,
    userId: DataTypes.INTEGER,
    categoryId: DataTypes.INTEGER
  });
  return Task;
};
```

Sample API endpoint

```javascript
// routes/tasks.js
router.post('/', async (req, res) => {
  try {
    const task = await Task.create({
      title: req.body.title,
      userId: req.user.id,
      completed: false
    });
    res.status(201).json(task);
  } catch (error) {
    res.status(500).json({ error: 'Error creating task' });
  }
});
```

Deploy the API using Azure CLI:

```
az webapp create \
  --resource-group CloudTaskerRG \
  --plan AppServicePlan \
  --name cloudtasker-api \
  --runtime "NODE|18-lts" \
```

```
--deployment-local-git
```

Push your code to the Git URL Azure provides.

Step 3: Building the Front-End

Technologies Used: React, Axios, React Router

Sample React Component:

```
// components/TaskList.js
import React, { useEffect, useState } from 'react';
import axios from 'axios';

const TaskList = () => {
  const [tasks, setTasks] = useState([]);

  useEffect(() => {
    axios.get('/api/tasks')
      .then(response => setTasks(response.data))
      .catch(err => console.error(err));
  }, []);

  return (
    <ul>
      {tasks.map(task => (
      <li key={task.id}>{task.title} {task.completed ? '✓' : ''}</li>
      ))}
    </ul>
  );
};

export default TaskList;
```

Deploy the front-end:

```
az webapp create \
  --resource-group CloudTaskerRG \
  --plan AppServicePlan \
  --name cloudtasker-client \
```

```
  --runtime "NODE|18-lts"
```

Configure build and deployment scripts as needed. Alternatively, host the front-end using Azure Static Web Apps.

Step 4: Enabling Authentication

Use **Azure AD B2C** for authentication:

1. Set up an Azure AD B2C tenant

2. Create a user flow (Sign up + Sign in)

3. Register front-end and back-end applications

4. Configure redirect URIs

5. Use MSAL.js in the front-end to authenticate

```javascript
import * as msal from "@azure/msal-browser";

const msalInstance = new msal.PublicClientApplication({
  auth: {
    clientId: "your-client-id",
    authority: "https://your-tenant.b2clogin.com/tfp/your-
tenant.onmicrosoft.com/B2C_1_signup_signin",
    redirectUri: "http://localhost:3000",
  }
});
```

Step 5: Using Azure Blob Storage

Create a blob container:

```
az storage account create \
  --name cloudtaskerstorage \
  --resource-group CloudTaskerRG \
  --location "East US" \
  --sku Standard_LRS
```

```
az storage container create \
  --name taskattachments \
  --account-name cloudtaskerstorage \
  --public-access off
```

In your back-end, use the `@azure/storage-blob` package to upload files:

```
const { BlobServiceClient } = require('@azure/storage-blob');

const uploadFile = async (fileBuffer, fileName) => {
  const blobServiceClient =
BlobServiceClient.fromConnectionString(process.env.AZURE_STORAGE_CON
NECTION_STRING);
  const containerClient =
blobServiceClient.getContainerClient("taskattachments");
  const blockBlobClient =
containerClient.getBlockBlobClient(fileName);
  await blockBlobClient.uploadData(fileBuffer);
};
```

Step 6: Setting Up CI/CD with Azure DevOps

1. Create a new project in Azure DevOps

2. Link your repository (GitHub or Azure Repos)

3. Create pipelines:

Sample `azure-pipelines.yml` **for the back-end**:

```
trigger:
- main

pool:
  vmImage: 'ubuntu-latest'

steps:
- task: NodeTool@0
  inputs:
    versionSpec: '18.x'
```

```yaml
    displayName: 'Install Node.js'

- script: |
    npm install
    npm test
  displayName: 'Install dependencies and run tests'

- task: AzureWebApp@1
  inputs:
    azureSubscription: 'My Azure Subscription'
    appName: 'cloudtasker-api'
    package: '.'
```

Step 7: Monitoring and Application Insights

Enable monitoring in your App Services:

```
az monitor app-insights component create \
  --app CloudTaskerInsights \
  --location "East US" \
  --resource-group CloudTaskerRG \
  --application-type web
```

Add the Application Insights SDK to your Node.js API:

```
npm install applicationinsights

const appInsights = require("applicationinsights");
appInsights.setup(process.env.APPINSIGHTS_INSTRUMENTATIONKEY).start(
);
```

This provides telemetry on requests, failures, dependencies, and performance.

Step 8: Managing Secrets with Key Vault

Use Azure Key Vault to store connection strings and API keys securely:

```
az keyvault create --name CloudTaskerVault --resource-group
CloudTaskerRG
```

```
az keyvault secret set --vault-name CloudTaskerVault --name
"SQLConnectionString" --value "your-connection-string"
```

In your app:

```
const { DefaultAzureCredential } = require("@azure/identity");
const { SecretClient } = require("@azure/keyvault-secrets");

const credential = new DefaultAzureCredential();
const client = new
SecretClient("https://cloudtaskervault.vault.azure.net",
credential);

const getSecret = async (name) => {
  const secret = await client.getSecret(name);
  return secret.value;
};
```

Conclusion

By following these steps, you've successfully developed and deployed a robust cloud-native task management app using Microsoft Azure. You've utilized core services like App Services, Azure SQL, Blob Storage, Azure AD B2C, Key Vault, and Application Insights — all of which integrate seamlessly for an efficient, scalable, and secure cloud solution.

This kind of architecture not only simplifies maintenance and scaling but also lays a strong foundation for future enhancements, such as mobile app integration, microservices, or AI-driven features using Azure Cognitive Services.

Deploying a Serverless Chatbot

In this section, we'll build and deploy a fully serverless chatbot using Microsoft Azure. This solution leverages Azure Functions, Azure Bot Service, Azure Cognitive Services (particularly Language Understanding - LUIS), and Azure Blob Storage. Our chatbot will be designed to answer frequently asked questions for a hypothetical e-commerce site and can be extended with custom functionality.

The project aims to be scalable, cost-effective, and easy to manage without the need to provision and maintain servers manually. All logic will execute on demand through serverless components.

Project Overview

We are developing a serverless chatbot named **ShopHelpBot**, designed to:

- Respond to customer inquiries using a natural language interface

- Use Azure Bot Service for conversation handling

- Utilize LUIS (Language Understanding Intelligent Service) for NLP

- Execute business logic via Azure Functions

- Store assets and logs in Azure Blob Storage

- Be deployable across websites, Teams, and mobile apps

This modular design allows for robust functionality, integration with other services, and minimal overhead in terms of maintenance.

Architecture

Components:

1. **Azure Bot Service** – Acts as the core communication hub

2. **LUIS** – Interprets user intents and extracts entities

3. **Azure Functions** – Executes custom logic in response to messages

4. **Azure Blob Storage** – Stores transcripts, logs, and assets

5. **Azure App Configuration / Key Vault** – Secures configuration

Flow:

User Message → Azure Bot → LUIS → Azure Function → Response → Azure Bot → User

---

Step 1: Creating the Bot Service

Create a new Bot Channel Registration via the Azure Portal or CLI:

```
az bot create \
```

```
--resource-group ShopHelpRG \
--name ShopHelpBot \
--kind registration \
--location "West Europe" \
--endpoint https://shophelp-api.azurewebsites.net/api/messages \
--sku F0
```

This creates a placeholder for the bot that we will connect to Azure Functions.

Step 2: Building Azure Functions for Chat Logic

Initialize a new Azure Functions project in Node.js or C#.

Example (Node.js):

```
func init ShopHelpBot --javascript
cd ShopHelpBot
func new --name chatbotHandler --template "HTTP trigger"
```

Sample function code:

```
module.exports = async function (context, req) {
  const intent = req.body.intent;
  let responseMessage = '';

  switch (intent) {
    case 'OrderStatus':
      responseMessage = "Please provide your order number.";
      break;
    case 'ReturnPolicy':
      responseMessage = "You can return items within 30 days.";
      break;
    default:
      responseMessage = "Sorry, I didn't understand that.";
  }

  context.res = {
    body: {
      reply: responseMessage
    }
```

```
    };
};
```

Deploy the function to Azure:

```
func azure functionapp publish shophelp-api
```

This function will be the webhook that Azure Bot Service calls when a user sends a message.

Step 3: Integrating with LUIS for Intent Recognition

Go to the LUIS portal and create a new app.

Add Intents:

- OrderStatus

- ReturnPolicy

- ProductAvailability

Add Utterances: For OrderStatus, examples include:

- "Where is my order?"

- "Track my order"

- "Order status for order number 1234"

Train and publish the app. Note your endpoint URL and authoring key.

Example LUIS result:

```
{
  "query": "Where is my order?",
  "prediction": {
    "topIntent": "OrderStatus",
    "intents": {
      "OrderStatus": {
        "score": 0.95
```

```
      }
    },
    "entities": {}
  }
}
```

Now update the Azure Function to include LUIS call logic using `axios` or `fetch`.

```
const axios = require('axios');

const getIntent = async (text) => {
  const response = await
axios.get(`https://westeurope.api.cognitive.microsoft.com/luis/predi
ction/v3.0/apps/YOUR_APP_ID/slots/production/predict`, {
    params: {
      'subscription-key': process.env.LUIS_KEY,
      'query': text
    }
  });
  return response.data.prediction.topIntent;
};
```

Step 4: Wiring Azure Bot Service to Azure Function

Go back to your Bot Channel Registration and set the **Messaging endpoint** to your Azure Function URL, e.g.:

```
https://shophelp-api.azurewebsites.net/api/chatbotHandler
```

The bot now sends messages to your function, which uses LUIS to determine intent and sends back a response.

Step 5: Adding Blob Storage for Chat Transcripts

Create a storage account and container:

```
az storage account create \
  --name shophelpstorage \
  --resource-group ShopHelpRG \
```

```
--location "West Europe" \
--sku Standard_LRS

az storage container create \
  --name transcripts \
  --account-name shophelpstorage \
  --public-access off
```

Save transcripts from the bot:

```
const { BlobServiceClient } = require('@azure/storage-blob');

const saveTranscript = async (conversationId, transcript) => {
  const blobServiceClient =
BlobServiceClient.fromConnectionString(process.env.STORAGE_CONNECTIO
N_STRING);
  const containerClient =
blobServiceClient.getContainerClient('transcripts');
  const blobClient =
containerClient.getBlockBlobClient(`${conversationId}.json`);
  await blobClient.upload(JSON.stringify(transcript),
Buffer.byteLength(JSON.stringify(transcript)));
};
```

Step 6: Securing Secrets with Azure Key Vault

Store secrets like LUIS keys and storage keys securely:

```
az keyvault create --name ShopHelpVault --resource-group ShopHelpRG
az keyvault secret set --vault-name ShopHelpVault --name "LUISKey" -
-value "your-luis-key"
az keyvault secret set --vault-name ShopHelpVault --name
"StorageConnStr" --value "your-storage-conn-str"
```

Access them in your Azure Functions using Managed Identity or Azure App Configuration.

Step 7: Deploying Channels (Web Chat, Teams, etc.)

Enable Web Chat:

1. In the Azure Portal, go to your bot resource

2. Click on "Channels" > "Web Chat" > Enable

3. Copy the embed code to your site:

```html
<script src="https://cdn.botframework.com/botframework-
webchat/latest/webchat.js"></script>
<div id="webchat" role="main"></div>
<script>
  window.WebChat.renderWebChat({
    directLine: window.WebChat.createDirectLine({ token:
'YOUR_DIRECT_LINE_TOKEN' })
  }, document.getElementById('webchat'));
</script>
```

Other Channels:

- Teams

- Slack

- Facebook Messenger

All can be configured via the Azure Portal under the "Channels" section.

Step 8: Monitoring with Application Insights

Enable monitoring on your Azure Function App:

```
az monitor app-insights component create \
  --app ShopHelpInsights \
  --location "West Europe" \
  --resource-group ShopHelpRG \
  --application-type web
```

Link the Application Insights instance to your function for performance and error tracking.

Add SDK code if needed:

```
const appInsights = require("applicationinsights");
```

```
appInsights.setup(process.env.APPINSIGHTS_INSTRUMENTATIONKEY).start(
);
```

Step 9: CI/CD Using GitHub Actions or Azure DevOps

Sample GitHub Action:

```
name: Deploy Chatbot Function

on:
  push:
    branches:
      - main

jobs:
  build-and-deploy:
    runs-on: ubuntu-latest
    steps:
      - uses: actions/checkout@v2

      - name: Set up Node.js
        uses: actions/setup-node@v2
        with:
          node-version: '18'

      - name: Install dependencies
        run: npm install

      - name: Azure Login
        uses: azure/login@v1
        with:
          creds: ${{ secrets.AZURE_CREDENTIALS }}

      - name: Deploy to Azure Functions
        run: |
          func azure functionapp publish shophelp-api
```

Use Azure DevOps pipelines for more complex multi-stage deployments.

Step 10: Extending and Maintaining

Now that your serverless chatbot is live, consider these enhancements:

- Add QnA Maker or Azure Cognitive Search for document-based responses

- Integrate CRM systems like Dynamics or Salesforce

- Use Cosmos DB to persist conversational state or user preferences

- Localize with Azure Translator

- Run A/B testing on response flows

Conclusion

You've now built a scalable, intelligent, serverless chatbot using Azure. From understanding intent with LUIS to managing logic with Azure Functions and enhancing the experience via Blob Storage and App Insights, the project shows how Azure empowers developers to deliver cutting-edge conversational interfaces with minimal infrastructure concerns.

The bot is extensible, secure, and capable of integrating with a wide array of channels and back-end systems. It's a powerful pattern you can replicate across support, sales, and other business domains.

Creating a Scalable E-commerce Backend

In this section, we will build a robust and scalable backend for a cloud-native e-commerce application using Microsoft Azure. The system will support product listing, inventory management, order processing, payment integration, and user account handling. Our architecture will be microservices-based, designed to scale horizontally, and decoupled via event-driven patterns to ensure resilience and maintainability.

The technologies and services used will include:

- Azure Kubernetes Service (AKS)

- Azure SQL Database and Cosmos DB

- Azure Service Bus

- Azure Blob Storage

- Azure Functions for lightweight tasks

- Azure API Management

- Azure Key Vault

- Azure Monitor and Application Insights

This implementation targets enterprise-grade solutions that can serve thousands of users concurrently and be easily extended with additional features such as recommendation engines or analytics.

Architecture Overview

The e-commerce backend will follow a distributed architecture:

1. **API Gateway** – Azure API Management for routing requests

2. **Microservices** – Deployed to AKS (Products, Orders, Users, Payments)

3. **Databases** – Azure SQL for transactional data, Cosmos DB for catalog

4. **Message Queue** – Azure Service Bus for communication between services

5. **Blob Storage** – For product images and receipts

6. **Function Apps** – For async tasks like sending confirmation emails

7. **Security** – Key Vault for credentials, RBAC, and Identity integration

Each microservice is independently deployable and uses a bounded context with its own data store.

Step 1: Provisioning the Kubernetes Cluster (AKS)

Create the AKS cluster:

```
az aks create \
  --resource-group EcommerceRG \
  --name EcommerceCluster \
  --node-count 3 \
  --enable-addons monitoring \
  --generate-ssh-keys
```

Connect to the cluster:

```
az aks get-credentials --resource-group EcommerceRG --name
EcommerceCluster
```

Step 2: Building Microservices

We'll use Node.js with Express and PostgreSQL for the Products and Orders services,
deployed in separate containers.

Products Service Example:

```javascript
const express = require('express');
const app = express();
const { Pool } = require('pg');

const pool = new Pool({
  user: 'admin',
  host: 'ecommerce-sql.postgres.database.azure.com',
  database: 'productsdb',
  password: process.env.DB_PASS,
  port: 5432,
  ssl: true
});

app.get('/products', async (req, res) => {
  const result = await pool.query('SELECT * FROM products');
  res.json(result.rows);
});

app.listen(3000, () => console.log('Products service running'));
```

Dockerfile:

```dockerfile
FROM node:18
WORKDIR /usr/src/app
COPY package*.json ./
RUN npm install
COPY . .
EXPOSE 3000
CMD ["node", "index.js"]
```

Step 3: Deploying to AKS

Create a Kubernetes Deployment and Service for each microservice:

```yaml
apiVersion: apps/v1
kind: Deployment
metadata:
  name: products-deployment
spec:
  replicas: 2
  selector:
    matchLabels:
      app: products
  template:
    metadata:
      labels:
        app: products
    spec:
      containers:
      - name: products
        image: myregistry.azurecr.io/products-service:latest
        ports:
        - containerPort: 3000
```

Expose with a service:

```yaml
apiVersion: v1
kind: Service
metadata:
  name: products-service
spec:
  type: ClusterIP
  selector:
    app: products
  ports:
  - port: 80
    targetPort: 3000
```

Repeat similarly for orders, users, and payments.

Step 4: Setting Up Databases

Azure SQL for Orders and Users

```
az sql server create \
  --name ecommerce-sql \
  --resource-group EcommerceRG \
  --location "East US" \
  --admin-user sqladmin \
  --admin-password P@ssw0rd123

az sql db create \
  --name OrdersDB \
  --server ecommerce-sql \
  --resource-group EcommerceRG \
  --service-objective S1
```

Cosmos DB for Product Catalog

```
az cosmosdb create \
  --name ecommercecosmos \
  --resource-group EcommerceRG \
  --kind MongoDB
```

Step 5: Integrating Azure Service Bus

Service Bus is used for handling asynchronous operations like order processing.

Create a namespace:

```
az servicebus namespace create \
  --resource-group EcommerceRG \
  --name EcommerceBus \
  --location "East US"
```

Add a queue:

```
az servicebus queue create \
  --resource-group EcommerceRG \
  --namespace-name EcommerceBus \
```

```
  --name orders-queue
```

Node.js Consumer (Order Processor):

```
const { ServiceBusClient } = require("@azure/service-bus");

const sbClient = new
ServiceBusClient(process.env.SERVICE_BUS_CONNECTION_STRING);
const receiver = sbClient.createReceiver("orders-queue");

const processMessage = async (message) => {
  console.log("Received order:", message.body);
  // Process order
};

receiver.subscribe({
  processMessage,
  processError: async (err) => console.error(err)
});
```

Step 6: Azure Functions for Background Tasks

Azure Functions are used for operations like emailing order confirmations.

Create a new function:

```
func init SendOrderEmail --javascript
cd SendOrderEmail
func new --name SendEmail --template "HTTP trigger"
```

Sample Code:

```
module.exports = async function (context, req) {
  const { to, subject, body } = req.body;
  // integrate with SendGrid or SMTP
  context.res = {
    status: 200,
    body: "Email sent"
  };
};
```

Deploy with:

```
func azure functionapp publish sendorderemail
```

Invoke this function asynchronously from the order microservice after queue processing.

Step 7: Using Blob Storage

Blob Storage holds product images, receipts, or invoices.

Create a storage account:

```
az storage account create \
  --name ecommercefiles \
  --resource-group EcommerceRG \
  --location "East US" \
  --sku Standard_LRS
```

Create a container:

```
az storage container create \
  --account-name ecommercefiles \
  --name product-images
```

Upload from Node.js:

```
const { BlobServiceClient } = require('@azure/storage-blob');

const uploadImage = async (buffer, name) => {
  const blobService =
BlobServiceClient.fromConnectionString(process.env.AZURE_STORAGE_CON
N_STRING);
  const container = blobService.getContainerClient("product-
images");
  const blockBlob = container.getBlockBlobClient(name);
  await blockBlob.uploadData(buffer);
};
```

Step 8: Secure Configuration with Key Vault

Store secrets centrally:

```
az keyvault create --name EcommerceVault --resource-group
EcommerceRG
az keyvault secret set --vault-name EcommerceVault --name
"DbPassword" --value "P@ssw0rd123"
```

Access in code:

```
const { DefaultAzureCredential } = require("@azure/identity");
const { SecretClient } = require("@azure/keyvault-secrets");

const client = new
SecretClient("https://ecommercevault.vault.azure.net", new
DefaultAzureCredential());
const dbPassword = await client.getSecret("DbPassword");
```

Step 9: API Gateway with Azure API Management

Create API Management instance:

```
az apim create \
  --name EcommerceAPI \
  --resource-group EcommerceRG \
  --publisher-name "Ecommerce Ltd" \
  --publisher-email "admin@ecommerce.com"
```

Import OpenAPI specs for each microservice and route requests like:

- api.ecommerce.com/products

- api.ecommerce.com/orders

- api.ecommerce.com/payments

Add policies for throttling, caching, and logging.

Step 10: Monitoring and Diagnostics

Enable Azure Monitor and Application Insights for services:

```
az monitor app-insights component create \
  --app EcommerceInsights \
  --location "East US" \
  --resource-group EcommerceRG \
  --application-type web
```

Integrate Application Insights SDK in microservices:

```
const appInsights = require("applicationinsights");
appInsights.setup(process.env.APPINSIGHTS_INSTRUMENTATION_KEY).start
();
```

Collect telemetry, diagnose failures, and set up alert rules for CPU, memory, and error rate.

Conclusion

You've now built a production-grade, scalable backend for an e-commerce application using Azure's cloud-native technologies. The system uses microservices on AKS, leverages managed databases and event-driven architecture via Service Bus, secures secrets with Key Vault, and provides robust monitoring and scalability features through native Azure tooling.

This backend is flexible, highly available, and ready for integration with front-end clients, mobile apps, and third-party systems. It serves as a strong template for any cloud-scale backend architecture.

Integrating Azure Cognitive Services

In this section, we'll explore how to enrich applications by integrating Azure Cognitive Services into a cloud-native environment. Azure Cognitive Services provide pre-built AI capabilities accessible via APIs and SDKs that enable applications to see, hear, speak, understand, and make decisions. These services can be used without requiring deep data science or machine learning knowledge.

We'll build a cloud-native application that integrates several Cognitive Services, including:

- Computer Vision (image recognition and tagging)

- Text Analytics (sentiment analysis and language detection)

- Translator (real-time translation)

- Speech-to-Text and Text-to-Speech (voice interaction)

- Azure OpenAI for advanced text generation

We will deploy these components on Azure using serverless technologies, with Azure Functions and Azure Logic Apps, and secure them using Azure Key Vault and Azure API Management. The app will be scalable, stateless, and event-driven.

Scenario: Smart Feedback Processing System

Our application, **SmartFeedback**, is a customer feedback intake and analysis platform. Customers can submit text, audio, or images. The backend uses Azure Cognitive Services to analyze sentiment, translate input if needed, recognize key objects in images, and convert speech to text. This is ideal for global businesses collecting user feedback from multiple channels and formats.

Step 1: Setting Up the Resource Group and Services

Create a resource group and provision the required Cognitive Services:

```
az group create --name SmartFeedbackRG --location "East US"
```

Create Cognitive Services resource:

```
az cognitiveservices account create \
  --name SmartFeedbackCognitive \
  --resource-group SmartFeedbackRG \
  --kind CognitiveServices \
  --sku S0 \
  --location "East US" \
  --yes
```

Enable specific services:

- Vision

- Language

- Translator

- Speech

You can also provision these as individual resources for better granularity and pricing control.

Step 2: Analyzing Text with Text Analytics

Text submitted through a form or API can be analyzed using the Text Analytics API.

Install the SDK:

```
npm install @azure/ai-text-analytics
```

Node.js example to analyze sentiment and language:

```
const { TextAnalyticsClient, AzureKeyCredential } =
require("@azure/ai-text-analytics");

const endpoint = process.env.TEXT_ANALYTICS_ENDPOINT;
const apiKey = process.env.TEXT_ANALYTICS_KEY;

const client = new TextAnalyticsClient(endpoint, new
AzureKeyCredential(apiKey));

const analyzeFeedback = async (text) => {
  const sentimentResult = await client.analyzeSentiment([text]);
  const languageResult = await client.detectLanguage([text]);
  return {
    sentiment: sentimentResult[0].sentiment,
    language: languageResult[0].primaryLanguage.name
  };
};
```

Integrate this in an Azure Function triggered by a POST request containing user feedback.

Step 3: Translating Text with Azure Translator

If the detected language isn't English, we'll translate it before analysis using Azure Translator.

API call using axios:

```
const axios = require('axios');

const translateText = async (text, fromLang, toLang = 'en') => {
  const endpoint = process.env.TRANSLATOR_ENDPOINT;
  const key = process.env.TRANSLATOR_KEY;

  const response = await axios.post(
    `${endpoint}/translate?api-
version=3.0&from=${fromLang}&to=${toLang}`,
    [{ Text: text }],
    {
      headers: {
        'Ocp-Apim-Subscription-Key': key,
        'Content-Type': 'application/json'
      }
    }
  );
  return response.data[0].translations[0].text;
};
```

Now integrate it with the text analysis logic so that all non-English inputs are first translated before processing.

Step 4: Speech-to-Text with Azure Speech Service

Handle audio input by transcribing it to text. This service is useful for voicemail feedback or audio file uploads.

Install the speech SDK:

```
npm install microsoft-cognitiveservices-speech-sdk
```

Example code:

```
const sdk = require("microsoft-cognitiveservices-speech-sdk");
```

```
const speechConfig =
sdk.SpeechConfig.fromSubscription(process.env.SPEECH_KEY,
process.env.SPEECH_REGION);
speechConfig.speechRecognitionLanguage = "en-US";

const audioConfig =
sdk.AudioConfig.fromWavFileInput(fs.readFileSync("feedback.wav"));

const recognizer = new sdk.SpeechRecognizer(speechConfig,
audioConfig);

recognizer.recognizeOnceAsync(result => {
  console.log(`Recognized: ${result.text}`);
});
```

Deploy this inside an Azure Function to automatically transcribe uploaded audio blobs.

Step 5: Image Processing with Computer Vision

For image-based feedback, such as screenshots or product pictures, we'll use the Computer Vision API to extract tags and text.

Install the SDK:

```
npm install @azure/cognitiveservices-computervision
```

Example usage:

```
const { ComputerVisionClient } = require("@azure/cognitiveservices-computervision");
const { CognitiveServicesCredentials } = require("@azure/ms-rest-azure-js");

const credentials = new
CognitiveServicesCredentials(process.env.VISION_KEY);
const client = new ComputerVisionClient(credentials,
process.env.VISION_ENDPOINT);

const analyzeImage = async (imageUrl) => {
  const result = await client.analyzeImage(imageUrl, {
visualFeatures: ["Description", "Tags", "Objects"] });
```

```
  return result;
};
```

You can use this function in response to a Blob Storage trigger when users upload image feedback.

Step 6: Generating Smart Summaries and Responses with Azure OpenAI

To automate response generation and summaries, we'll use Azure OpenAI (based on GPT models).

Create the Azure OpenAI resource and deploy a model (e.g., gpt-35-turbo).

Call the OpenAI endpoint:

```
const axios = require('axios');

const generateResponse = async (summaryText) => {
  const response = await axios.post(
    `${process.env.OPENAI_ENDPOINT}/openai/deployments/gpt-35-
turbo/chat/completions?api-version=2023-03-15-preview`,
    {
      messages: [
        { role: "system", content: "You are a helpful feedback
analyst." },
        { role: "user", content: `Summarize and generate a response
to this feedback: ${summaryText}` }
      ]
    },
    {
      headers: {
        'api-key': process.env.OPENAI_KEY,
        'Content-Type': 'application/json'
      }
    }
  );

  return response.data.choices[0].message.content;
};
```

Use this in conjunction with sentiment and language analysis to generate automated, context-aware replies.

Step 7: Logic App for Workflow Automation

Use Azure Logic Apps to tie all services together visually.

Example Logic App flow:

1. HTTP trigger receives feedback

2. If input is audio → call Speech-to-Text

3. If input is image → call Computer Vision

4. If input is text or transcribed → detect language

5. Translate if not English

6. Analyze sentiment

7. Generate response via OpenAI

8. Store all results in Blob Storage

9. Notify support team or CRM

Step 8: Securing the Application with Azure Key Vault

Store all sensitive API keys in Key Vault:

```
az keyvault create --name SmartFeedbackVault --resource-group
SmartFeedbackRG

az keyvault secret set --vault-name SmartFeedbackVault --name
"TextAnalyticsKey" --value "KEY_HERE"
az keyvault secret set --vault-name SmartFeedbackVault --name
"OpenAIKey" --value "KEY_HERE"
```

Retrieve in code:

```
const { DefaultAzureCredential } = require("@azure/identity");
const { SecretClient } = require("@azure/keyvault-secrets");

const credential = new DefaultAzureCredential();
const client = new
SecretClient("https://smartfeedbackvault.vault.azure.net",
credential);

const openAIKey = await client.getSecret("OpenAIKey");
```

Step 9: Monitoring with Azure Application Insights

Add Application Insights to all Functions and services:

```
az monitor app-insights component create \
  --app SmartFeedbackInsights \
  --location "East US" \
  --resource-group SmartFeedbackRG \
  --application-type web
```

Enable distributed tracing, log retention, and performance metrics.

Conclusion

This project demonstrates the power and flexibility of Azure Cognitive Services when integrated into a modern, cloud-native architecture. By combining services like Text Analytics, Translator, Speech, Computer Vision, and OpenAI, developers can create highly intelligent applications capable of processing diverse forms of user feedback at scale.

Through the use of serverless components like Azure Functions and Logic Apps, the system remains lightweight and responsive. Additionally, it is easily extensible to include other capabilities such as facial recognition, knowledge mining, or even integration with Power BI for analytics dashboards. SmartFeedback is a blueprint for building intelligent, automated, and multilingual digital experiences.

Chapter 10: Moving Forward with Azure

Microsoft Certifications and Learning Paths

As cloud computing continues to dominate the technology landscape, developers and IT professionals must not only stay up-to-date with rapidly evolving tools but also demonstrate their expertise. Microsoft Azure provides a vast ecosystem, and gaining official certification is an excellent way to validate your knowledge and accelerate your career. In this section, we'll explore the certifications available, outline learning paths, offer study resources, and guide you through the steps to becoming an Azure-certified professional.

Why Certifications Matter

Microsoft certifications offer several benefits:

- **Career Advancement**: Certified professionals often have access to better job opportunities and higher salaries.

- **Structured Learning**: Certifications help structure your learning and ensure you're covering essential topics.

- **Credibility**: They provide a trusted, third-party validation of your skills.

- **Community Recognition**: Certifications position you as a thought leader or go-to person within your teams.

Whether you're a beginner or an experienced developer, there's a certification path tailored to your level and career goals.

Azure Certification Tracks

Microsoft offers certifications in several domains, categorized into **Fundamentals**, **Associate**, **Expert**, and **Specialty** levels.

Fundamentals

The **Azure Fundamentals (AZ-900)** certification is ideal for those who are new to Azure. It covers:

- Cloud computing concepts

- Core Azure services

- Security and compliance features

- Azure pricing and support

This is a non-technical certification, suitable even for sales and business professionals who want to understand the Azure landscape.

Associate

Once you're comfortable with the basics, you can progress to associate-level certifications:

- **Azure Developer Associate (AZ-204)**
  For software developers with at least one year of experience designing and building cloud-based applications. Skills measured include:

  - Developing Azure compute solutions (App Services, Functions, Containers)

  - Implementing Azure security

  - Integrating caching and content delivery

  - Connecting to and consuming Azure services and third-party services

- **Azure Administrator Associate (AZ-104)**
  Targeted at professionals who manage cloud services including storage, networking, and security.

Expert

The **Azure Solutions Architect Expert (AZ-305)** certification is suitable for those with advanced knowledge of designing cloud and hybrid solutions. Candidates should have experience with:

- Compute, network, storage, and security design

- Governance and compliance

- Business continuity strategies

This exam builds upon AZ-104, although it's not mandatory to complete AZ-104 first.

Specialty

Specialty certifications allow you to dive deep into niche areas:

- **Azure AI Engineer Associate (AI-102)**

- **Azure Data Scientist Associate (DP-100)**

- **Azure IoT Developer (AZ-220)**

- **Azure Security Engineer Associate (AZ-500)**

Each of these certifications is geared towards a specific skill set and job role.

Choosing Your Path

Your path should align with your career goals. Here's a decision matrix to help you decide:

- **Want to prove foundational knowledge?** Start with AZ-900.

- **Primarily a developer?** AZ-204 is the most relevant.

- **More interested in infrastructure and deployment?** Consider AZ-104.

- **Planning to lead architecture and strategy?** Aim for AZ-305.

- **Working with AI, data, or IoT?** Choose a specialty certification.

Learning Resources

Microsoft provides **free learning paths** via Microsoft Learn, which include interactive exercises, sandbox environments, and assessments.

Key Microsoft Learn Paths:

- **Azure Fundamentals**
  https://learn.microsoft.com/en-us/training/paths/azure-fundamentals/

- **Developing Solutions for Microsoft Azure (AZ-204)**
  https://learn.microsoft.com/en-us/training/paths/develop-microsoft-azure/

- **Designing Azure Infrastructure Solutions (AZ-305)**
  https://learn.microsoft.com/en-us/training/paths/design-azure-infrastructure/

In addition to Microsoft Learn, consider the following:

- **Pluralsight** – Offers in-depth Azure training videos.

- **LinkedIn Learning** – Certification-focused video tutorials.

- **Whizlabs, ExamPro, Udemy** – Offer exam simulators and practice tests.

Preparing for Certification Exams

Preparation strategy:

1. **Set a Goal Date**: Register for the exam to motivate yourself.

2. **Follow a Study Plan**: Break the material into manageable sections.

3. **Use Practice Exams**: Test your readiness and identify gaps.

4. **Join Study Groups**: Online forums and Discord communities can offer support.

5. **Hands-on Practice**: Use the Azure free tier to create and deploy services.

Example practice:

```
# Log in to Azure via CLI
az login

# Create a resource group
az group create --name MyResourceGroup --location eastus

# Deploy a web app
az webapp up --name mytestwebapp123 --resource-group MyResourceGroup
--runtime "NODE|18-lts"
```

Maintaining Certifications

Microsoft certifications are valid for one year. Renewal is free and involves passing a short online assessment through Microsoft Learn. Set reminders and keep learning through official modules to stay ahead.

Real-World Applications of Certifications

Case Study 1: A front-end developer in a fintech company pursued the AZ-204 and transitioned into a full-stack cloud engineer role within six months. Their understanding of Azure Functions and Cosmos DB enabled them to lead a serverless project.

Case Study 2: A sysadmin prepared for and passed AZ-104 and AZ-305. This led to a promotion to Cloud Solutions Architect, where they designed hybrid cloud strategies using Azure Arc and ExpressRoute.

Community and Support

- **Microsoft Tech Community**: Connect with experts and get answers to your questions.

- **Reddit (r/Azure)**: Community discussions, exam tips, and news.

- **Twitter**: Follow hashtags like #Azure #MSCert to keep up with announcements.

Consider joining the **Microsoft Learn Student Ambassadors** or attending **Microsoft Ignite** for networking and continuous growth.

Conclusion

Earning a Microsoft Azure certification is more than just a resume booster—it opens doors to innovation, leadership, and continuous learning. Whether you are looking to specialize in development, architecture, AI, or security, there's a certification tailored for you. Start your journey with a learning path that suits your goals, get hands-on with Azure services, and validate your expertise with industry-recognized credentials. By committing to ongoing education and leveraging community support, you'll stay at the forefront of cloud technology and position yourself for long-term success.

Joining the Azure Developer Community

Building a career in cloud development goes far beyond individual skill acquisition. To truly thrive in today's evolving tech landscape, developers must become active participants in a broader ecosystem. The Azure Developer Community offers immense opportunities for growth, networking, and collaboration. In this section, we explore the various ways to get involved, the platforms and programs that support developers, and how community engagement can enhance both your skills and your career.

The Importance of Community in Cloud Development

Involvement in the developer community can lead to:

- **Faster Learning**: Sharing knowledge and solving problems collectively accelerates learning.

- **Professional Networking**: Connecting with peers, mentors, and industry leaders opens doors to collaboration and career opportunities.

- **Recognition and Impact**: Publishing tutorials, contributing to open source, or speaking at events raises your professional profile.

- **Staying Current**: Communities are often the first to explore and share knowledge about new Azure features or industry trends.

Microsoft and the broader Azure ecosystem provide extensive support for developer communities. Whether you're an introverted coder or an extroverted tech evangelist, there's a place for you.

Official Microsoft Communities and Programs

Microsoft Learn Community

The Microsoft Learn Community provides an integrated hub where developers can:

- Participate in discussions

- Attend live virtual events and webinars

- Join regional or global user groups

- Contribute to GitHub learning repos

Visit: https://learn.microsoft.com/community

Microsoft Q&A

This is a dedicated platform where developers can ask technical questions and receive expert responses directly from Microsoft employees, MVPs (Most Valuable Professionals), and other seasoned developers.

Example query:

> How do I connect an Azure Function to a Cosmos DB instance using managed identity?

This encourages best practices and clarifies edge cases beyond standard documentation.

GitHub Discussions and Azure SDK Repos

Many Azure SDKs, tools, and services have their own GitHub repositories with active issue tracking and discussions. These are excellent places to:

- Report bugs

- Suggest enhancements

- Understand roadmap priorities

- Participate in open-source contributions

Example repo: https://github.com/Azure/azure-sdk-for-js

Community Recognition: Microsoft MVP Program

The **Microsoft Most Valuable Professional (MVP)** award is given to individuals who demonstrate exceptional leadership and sharing in technical communities. This includes:

- Writing blogs or tutorials

- Speaking at conferences or meetups

- Creating YouTube or Twitch content

- Contributing to open-source Azure tools

Being an MVP provides early access to Microsoft technologies, direct engagement with product teams, and invitations to exclusive events like the MVP Summit.

How to Become an MVP

There's no fixed application process. Instead, candidates are nominated by Microsoft employees or existing MVPs. To get noticed:

1. **Document your contributions** – Consistency is key.

2. **Share your journey publicly** – Use LinkedIn, Twitter, or Medium.

3. **Engage with your audience** – Answer comments, promote discussion.

4. **Collaborate and mentor** – Help others grow in their journey.

Community-Driven Events and Conferences

Microsoft Ignite

Ignite is one of the largest Microsoft events, featuring new announcements, deep-dive sessions, and expert panels. It includes hands-on labs and live Q&A with Azure engineering teams.

Sign up at: https://ignite.microsoft.com

Global Azure

Global Azure is a worldwide community-driven event held in multiple cities each year. It's ideal for:

- Participating in workshops and hackathons

- Meeting local Azure enthusiasts

- Presenting your own Azure projects or solutions

Azure Dev Camps

These are deep technical training sessions organized by Microsoft and partners. Developers learn about:

- Developing cloud-native applications

- Working with Azure Functions and Logic Apps

- Securing APIs using Azure AD and OAuth

Getting Involved in Online Communities

Online engagement offers a flexible way to contribute and grow. Here are a few prominent platforms:

Stack Overflow

Tag your questions or answers with `azure`, `azure-functions`, `azure-devops`, etc. This not only helps others but builds your own reputation over time.

Reddit

Subreddits such as r/AZURE and r/devops are active with technical questions, discussions, and job opportunities.

Twitter and LinkedIn

Follow and engage with influencers like:

- Scott Hanselman – @shanselman

- Donovan Brown – @DonovanBrown

- Christina Warren – @film_girl

Use hashtags: #Azure, #Serverless, #AzureDevOps, #CloudNative

---

Open Source Contributions

Contributing to open source is one of the most impactful ways to participate. Azure has many open-source tools and SDKs on GitHub. Getting started typically involves:

Cloning the repo:

```
git clone https://github.com/Azure/azure-sdk-for-js.git
cd azure-sdk-for-js
```

1.

Creating a feature branch:

```
git checkout -b feature/my-enhancement
```

2.
3. **Submitting a pull request:**

   - Include a clear title and description

   - Reference any related issues

   - Follow the project's contribution guidelines

Suggested Projects to Explore

- Azure/azure-cli

- Azure/azure-quickstart-templates

- Azure/azure-functions-host

Building Your Presence

Start a Blog or YouTube Channel

Share your Azure journey with the world:

- **Tutorials** – How-tos for deploying services or solving common issues.

- **Project Showcases** – Demonstrate real-world implementations.

- **Opinion Pieces** – Compare Azure with AWS or GCP, discuss trends.

Use free platforms like Dev.to, Medium, or Hashnode, or build your own with GitHub Pages.

Example Blog Post Ideas

- "How I Migrated a Monolith to Azure App Services"

- "Using Azure Key Vault for API Secrets"

- "Deploying a Serverless Backend in Under 10 Minutes"

Mentorship and Local Meetups

If you're looking to mentor or be mentored, joining or starting local Azure meetups is a great way to connect in real life. Meetup.com hosts many Azure groups across major cities. These meetups often feature:

- Technical sessions

- Career panels

- Hackathons and team challenges

Also consider joining student-focused groups like the **Microsoft Learn Student Ambassadors**, which offer resources for mentoring and leadership development.

Real-World Examples of Community Impact

Story 1: An aspiring developer started blogging about her Azure learning path and eventually caught the attention of a Microsoft recruiter. She's now working as a Cloud Solutions Engineer at a Fortune 500 company.

Story 2: A hobbyist contributor to Azure CLI GitHub repo was later invited to speak at Global Azure about CLI scripting best practices. He's now a recognized name in the open-source space.

Conclusion

Joining the Azure Developer Community is a strategic step for any cloud professional. Beyond acquiring certifications or mastering individual services, community engagement helps you learn faster, get noticed, and collaborate on cutting-edge solutions. From blogging and GitHub contributions to attending meetups or speaking at global events, every form of participation builds your brand and accelerates your growth. Whether you're just starting or already an expert, the Azure community is a powerful network ready to support and amplify your journey. Dive in, contribute, and become part of a global force shaping the future of cloud technology.

Exploring Advanced Azure Features

Once you've mastered the core services and gained confidence deploying, scaling, and securing applications in Microsoft Azure, the next natural step is to dive into advanced features that can elevate your solutions to the enterprise level. These features allow you to integrate cutting-edge technologies, optimize operations, improve resilience, and unlock innovative use cases. In this section, we'll explore advanced services and capabilities such as hybrid cloud integration, private networking, automation, AI/ML services, confidential computing, and advanced developer tooling.

Hybrid Cloud and Edge Computing

Azure enables seamless integration between on-premises systems and cloud infrastructure through a suite of hybrid services. This is ideal for businesses that require:

- Data sovereignty

- Low-latency processing

- Existing hardware investment utilization

- Regulatory compliance

Azure Arc

Azure Arc allows you to manage resources across environments—on-premises, multi-cloud, and edge—from a single control plane.

Key features include:

- Unified management for VMs, Kubernetes clusters, and databases

- Policy enforcement using Azure Policy

- Role-based access control across all connected resources

Example CLI setup to onboard a Kubernetes cluster with Azure Arc:

```
az login
az account set --subscription "<subscription_id>"
az connectedk8s connect --name myAKSCluster --resource-group
myResourceGroup
```

Azure Stack

Azure Stack extends Azure services to your datacenter or remote locations. It comes in different flavors:

- **Azure Stack Hub**: For fully disconnected or edge deployments

- **Azure Stack HCI**: For hyper-converged infrastructure

- **Azure Stack Edge**: For AI and compute-intensive tasks at the edge

---

Advanced Networking

Enterprise-grade applications often require highly available, secure, and optimized network architectures.

Private Link and Service Endpoints

Azure Private Link provides private connectivity to Azure services from your virtual network, keeping traffic off the public internet. This is essential for financial, government, or healthcare applications.

Example to create a Private Endpoint:

```
az network private-endpoint create \
  --name myPrivateEndpoint \
  --resource-group myResourceGroup \
  --vnet-name myVNet \
  --subnet mySubnet \
  --private-connection-resource-id
"/subscriptions/<sub_id>/resourceGroups/<rg>/providers/Microsoft.Sto
rage/storageAccounts/<storage_account>" \
  --group-id blob \
  --connection-name myConnection
```

Azure Front Door and Traffic Manager

Azure Front Door is a global, scalable entry point for your web applications, offering:

- SSL offloading

- Layer 7 routing

- Web Application Firewall (WAF)

Traffic Manager provides DNS-based traffic routing based on:

- Performance

- Geographic location

- Weighted distribution

Use these services to ensure low-latency experiences and global failover capabilities.

Serverless at Scale

Serverless architectures offer exceptional scalability, cost-efficiency, and rapid iteration. While Azure Functions and Logic Apps are commonly used, advanced scenarios include:

Durable Functions

Durable Functions enable stateful workflows in serverless apps. You can write orchestrators using code, define checkpoints, and manage retries.

Example pattern:

```javascript
const df = require("durable-functions");

module.exports = df.orchestrator(function* (context) {
  const output1 = yield context.df.callActivity("TaskA",
context.bindingData.input);
  const output2 = yield context.df.callActivity("TaskB", output1);
  return yield context.df.callActivity("TaskC", output2);
});
```

Event Grid and Event-Driven Architectures

Use Event Grid to subscribe to events from services like Blob Storage or custom apps. This enables real-time workflows and responsive systems.

Artificial Intelligence and Machine Learning

Azure makes it easy to integrate AI/ML features into your applications without becoming a data scientist.

Azure Cognitive Services

These are pre-built APIs for vision, speech, language, and decision-making:

- Face recognition

- Speech-to-text

- Sentiment analysis

- Personalizer for real-time recommendations

Example using Azure Text Analytics (Python):

```python
from azure.ai.textanalytics import TextAnalyticsClient
from azure.core.credentials import AzureKeyCredential

endpoint = "https://<your-endpoint>.cognitiveservices.azure.com/"
key = "<your-key>"

client = TextAnalyticsClient(endpoint=endpoint,
credential=AzureKeyCredential(key))
```

```
documents = ["Azure is a great cloud platform."]
response = client.analyze_sentiment(documents=documents)[0]
print("Sentiment:", response.sentiment)
```

Azure Machine Learning Service

Use Azure ML for building, training, and deploying models at scale.

Key capabilities:

- Automated ML (AutoML)

- ML pipelines and model versioning

- Compute clusters and managed endpoints

- Integration with Jupyter, VS Code, and GitHub

You can also register models and expose them via REST APIs for real-time predictions.

Security and Governance Enhancements

Beyond basic RBAC and policies, advanced features include:

Azure Policy as Code

Define infrastructure rules using JSON or initiatives, then deploy via CI/CD pipelines for consistent compliance.

Example policy to restrict VM sizes:

```
{
  "if": {
    "allOf": [
      {
        "field": "type",
        "equals": "Microsoft.Compute/virtualMachines"
      },
      {
        "field": "Microsoft.Compute/virtualMachines/sku.name",
        "notIn": ["Standard_DS1_v2", "Standard_DS2_v2"]
      }
    ]
```

```
  },
  "then": {
    "effect": "deny"
  }  .
}
```

Microsoft Defender for Cloud

Offers posture management, threat protection, and compliance reporting across:

- Azure

- AWS

- GCP

- On-premises workloads

Advanced use cases include Just-In-Time VM access, file integrity monitoring, and adaptive application controls.

Automation and DevOps

Automate deployments, testing, and management at scale with these tools:

Azure Bicep

Bicep is a domain-specific language (DSL) for ARM templates with improved syntax.

Example:

```
resource storage 'Microsoft.Storage/storageAccounts@2022-05-01' = {
  name: 'myuniquestorageacct'
  location: resourceGroup().location
  sku: {
    name: 'Standard_LRS'
  }
  kind: 'StorageV2'
  properties: {}
}
```

Azure DevOps Advanced Features

Azure DevOps offers:

- Multi-stage YAML pipelines

- Artifact feeds and container registries

- Release gates and approvals

- Integration with Azure Key Vault for secrets management

Use Azure DevOps REST APIs to programmatically manage builds and releases.

Observability and Analytics

Scaling apps in production requires robust observability.

Azure Monitor and Log Analytics

Aggregate metrics and logs from all services. Create queries with Kusto Query Language (KQL):

```
AzureDiagnostics
| where ResourceType == "APPLICATIONGATEWAYS"
| summarize count() by bin(TimeGenerated, 5m), requestUri_s
```

Application Insights

Provides deep performance telemetry including:

- Dependency tracking

- Live metrics stream

- Smart error diagnostics

- Usage analytics

Integrate with SDKs or auto-instrument via Azure App Services.

Confidential Computing

For high-security applications, Azure offers confidential computing using Trusted Execution Environments (TEEs). These protect data while in use.

Supported on:

- DC-series VMs with Intel SGX

- Azure Kubernetes Service using confidential containers

Use cases:

- Secure multi-party computation

- Financial modeling with confidential data

- Privacy-preserving analytics

Real-World Advanced Scenarios

Case Study 1: Hybrid Healthcare Platform

A healthcare provider used Azure Arc to manage patient data across 5 hospitals and centralize analytics in the cloud while maintaining GDPR compliance.

Case Study 2: Real-Time Analytics in Retail

A retail company used Event Grid + Azure Functions to process millions of transactions per hour and generate insights with Azure Synapse Analytics.

Case Study 3: FinTech API Platform

A financial services startup deployed a high-security API gateway using Azure Front Door, Private Link, and confidential computing, enabling PCI DSS compliance.

Conclusion

Exploring advanced Azure features unlocks a new tier of capability, allowing developers to design resilient, secure, performant, and innovative applications. Whether you're integrating AI, building hybrid architectures, automating complex workflows, or securing sensitive data with confidential computing, Azure provides the tools to bring enterprise-grade solutions to life. Mastering these advanced services empowers you to deliver scalable and cutting-edge systems that meet modern digital demands. Push beyond the fundamentals and start architecting the future with Azure.

Staying Up-to-Date with Azure

The world of cloud computing is evolving rapidly, and staying current with the latest features, best practices, and services offered by Azure is crucial for any developer or IT professional. As new capabilities are introduced and the platform grows, ensuring that you have the knowledge and skills to leverage Azure's full potential will set you apart in an ever-competitive industry. This section covers practical strategies to stay up-to-date with Azure, from using Microsoft's official resources to engaging with community-driven content and attending events that can help you stay ahead.

The Importance of Continuous Learning in Cloud Computing

Cloud computing is continuously evolving, with new technologies, tools, and methodologies being introduced at a rapid pace. Azure is no exception. Staying up-to-date not only helps in maintaining the functionality and security of applications but also ensures that you can make the most of new features and innovations. Here's why staying current is so important:

- **Innovation**: Azure constantly rolls out new features that can improve the performance, security, and scalability of your applications.

- **Security**: Keeping up with the latest patches and features ensures your applications stay secure against emerging threats.

- **Efficiency**: New updates often come with optimizations that can help reduce costs and improve performance.

- **Professional Development**: Being aware of new features can help you remain competitive in the job market and contribute meaningfully to your organization.

In cloud computing, ignoring updates can result in using outdated tools that no longer serve the most efficient or secure solutions. Thus, continuous learning is essential.

Official Microsoft Resources for Staying Current

The first and most reliable place to stay updated with Azure's latest features is through official Microsoft resources. Microsoft provides a plethora of resources to help developers, IT professionals, and businesses stay informed about the latest tools, services, and best practices.

Microsoft Learn

Microsoft Learn is an invaluable resource that offers free, interactive learning paths and modules. The platform is constantly updated with new content, including courses, tutorials, and hands-on labs on various Azure services. The topics range from beginner-level content to advanced topics like AI and security.

You can track your progress and even earn certifications as you go through these learning paths.

Key features:

- Interactive, hands-on labs

- Skills-based learning paths

- Real-time updates on new Azure features

- Integration with Microsoft Certifications

Visit: https://learn.microsoft.com/en-us/training/

Azure Blog

The Azure blog is another excellent resource for staying up-to-date. The blog provides announcements, case studies, and in-depth articles on new services and features, use cases, and how-to guides. It's the first place to check for news on upcoming Azure features, product updates, and important releases.

Key categories:

- **New product features**: Updates on newly released services or enhancements to existing services.

- **Customer success stories**: Learn how other organizations are using Azure to meet their needs.

- **Tech insights**: Thought leadership articles from Azure experts.

Visit: https://techcommunity.microsoft.com/t5/azure/ct-p/Azure

Azure Release Notes

The official release notes are the go-to resource for tracking the newest capabilities available in Azure. Release notes include detailed changelogs for each service, so you can quickly learn about new features, improvements, and bug fixes.

To stay current:

- Regularly check the **Azure updates page** to follow changes by service.

- Subscribe to the **Azure updates RSS feed** to receive immediate notifications on new changes.

Visit: https://azure.microsoft.com/en-us/updates/

Engaging with the Community

Community-driven resources are essential for gaining insights, learning from others, and exploring how people are using Azure in real-world scenarios. Engaging with the community provides exposure to different perspectives and keeps you informed about the latest trends and discussions around Azure.

Stack Overflow

Stack Overflow is an active platform where developers ask questions, provide answers, and discuss common challenges. By following the `azure` tag, you can stay updated with the latest issues and solutions that developers are encountering in the Azure ecosystem.

Additionally, many times, you will find solutions to problems and best practices that are not officially documented but have been tested by the community.

Visit: https://stackoverflow.com/questions/tagged/azure

Reddit

Subreddits like **r/Azure**, **r/Cloud**, and **r/AzureDevOps** are great spaces to find discussions on recent updates, troubleshooting tips, tutorials, and other cloud-related topics. Reddit's real-time conversation format makes it easy to stay updated and interact with professionals and enthusiasts alike.

Engage with threads such as:

- Discussions on new features and releases

- Troubleshooting guides

- User experiences with new Azure services

Visit: https://www.reddit.com/r/AZURE/

Twitter and LinkedIn

Following Azure-related hashtags such as **#Azure**, **#CloudComputing**, **#AzureDevOps**, and **#AzureUpdates** on Twitter is another way to stay informed. Many Azure engineers and Microsoft MVPs share real-time updates, tips, and announcements.

On LinkedIn, follow Azure product managers, engineers, and thought leaders to get updates directly from the people behind Azure.

Key accounts to follow:

- **@Azure**

- **@ScottGu**

- **@DonovanBrown**

Engage in conversations and ask questions to learn from others.

Attending Azure Events and Webinars

One of the best ways to stay up-to-date with Azure is by attending live events, webinars, and conferences. These events are where the latest features and best practices are often first announced and demonstrated.

Microsoft Ignite

Microsoft Ignite is an annual event that provides a deep dive into Microsoft's latest technologies, with a strong focus on Azure. This event brings together experts from around the world and features hundreds of sessions, workshops, and demos.

At Ignite, you can learn about:

- New Azure services and features

- Best practices from Azure architects and engineers

- Real-world case studies

Visit: https://ignite.microsoft.com

Global Azure

Global Azure is an annual community-led event that takes place in many cities around the world. It's a great way to meet fellow Azure enthusiasts and participate in hackathons, workshops, and lectures.

Global Azure features:

- Local meetups and speaker sessions

- Community-driven sessions on Azure best practices

- Networking with other Azure users and professionals

Visit: https://globalazure.net

Azure Webinars

Microsoft offers webinars regularly throughout the year on different topics related to Azure. These webinars are typically free to attend and often cover:

- New features and updates

- Best practices for specific services (like Azure Functions, Azure AI, etc.)

- Hands-on workshops

Visit: https://learn.microsoft.com/en-us/events/

Leveraging Azure Insider Programs

Azure offers several insider programs that allow developers and IT professionals to preview new features and services before they are generally available. These programs provide access to early versions of tools and services, as well as opportunities to influence product development by providing feedback.

Azure Preview Portal

The Azure Preview Portal provides early access to new services and features before they are released to the public. By opting into the Preview Portal, you can experiment with new features and contribute feedback directly to Microsoft.

Azure FastTrack

Azure FastTrack helps businesses deploy Azure at scale with guidance and best practices from Microsoft engineers. Through this program, you can gain early access to certain features and receive expert guidance on implementing them effectively.

Following Azure Roadmaps and Planning Your Development Strategy

To stay proactive rather than reactive, it's important to understand where Azure is heading. Microsoft publishes Azure product roadmaps to help users plan their cloud strategies and anticipate future changes in Azure services.

The Azure roadmap includes:

- Upcoming features and timelines

- Beta and preview services

- Retired services

By staying on top of the roadmap, you can begin planning for major changes in your applications ahead of time.

Visit: https://azure.microsoft.com/en-us/updates/

Conclusion

Staying up-to-date with Azure requires a commitment to ongoing learning and engagement with both official and community-driven resources. Microsoft's official sites like Azure Learn and the Azure Blog are invaluable for tracking new features and best practices. At the same time, engaging with community forums, attending events, and leveraging insider programs offer hands-on experience with upcoming changes. By combining these resources, you'll be well-positioned to leverage the full potential of Azure and stay ahead of the curve in an ever-evolving cloud landscape.

Chapter 11: Appendices

Glossary of Terms

Cloud computing and Azure development include a variety of specialized terms and acronyms. Understanding these terms thoroughly can significantly improve comprehension and efficiency when working within Microsoft Azure. This glossary provides clear, concise explanations and definitions to aid users at all experience levels.

A

Azure Active Directory (Azure AD)
A cloud-based identity and access management service by Microsoft that helps employees sign in and access resources.

Azure App Service
A platform-as-a-service (PaaS) that hosts web applications, REST APIs, and mobile backends without needing to manage underlying infrastructure.

Azure CLI (Command Line Interface)
A command-line tool providing scripts for managing Azure resources, suitable for automation tasks.

Azure Cognitive Services
A set of APIs and SDKs that allows developers to build intelligent applications without direct AI or data science expertise.

Azure Cosmos DB
A fully-managed NoSQL database service for modern app development, supporting various data models and APIs.

Azure DevOps
A suite of development tools, services, and practices facilitating collaboration, CI/CD pipelines, code management, and project management.

Azure Functions
Serverless computing services provided by Azure, designed to allow running small pieces of code or functions triggered by specific events.

Azure Monitor
Provides comprehensive monitoring solutions for Azure resources, including metrics, diagnostics, and logs, allowing efficient troubleshooting and alert management.

Azure Resource Manager (ARM)
A management service that enables organizing, deploying, and managing Azure resources using declarative templates and REST APIs.

B

Blob Storage
A service for storing massive amounts of unstructured data, such as text or binary data.

C

CI/CD (Continuous Integration/Continuous Deployment)
A development practice where code changes are automatically tested, integrated, and deployed to a production environment.

Cloud-Native Application
Applications explicitly designed for the cloud environment, optimized to leverage cloud infrastructure and services.

Containerization
A virtualization method used to package applications with their dependencies, ensuring consistent environments across development and deployment stages.

D

Docker
An open-source tool for containerizing applications, enabling consistent deployment and execution across various environments.

Deployment Slot
A feature within Azure App Services allowing multiple versions of an application to run simultaneously for testing and seamless upgrades.

F

Fault Tolerance
The capability of a system to continue operating properly in the event of failure of one or more components.

I

Infrastructure as a Service (IaaS)
Cloud computing service model providing virtualized hardware resources such as computing power, storage, and networking.

K

Kubernetes
An open-source platform for managing containerized workloads and services, providing automation for deployment, scaling, and operations.

L

Load Balancer
A service distributing incoming network traffic across multiple servers or virtual machines to ensure reliability and performance.

M

Microservices
An architectural approach to building applications composed of independently deployable services, each performing specific functions.

N

NoSQL Database
Databases optimized for storing and retrieving data without a rigid relational schema, offering scalability and flexibility.

P

Platform as a Service (PaaS)
Cloud computing model offering a development environment where users can build, deploy, and manage applications without dealing directly with underlying infrastructure.

PowerShell
A scripting language and command-line shell from Microsoft used for automating tasks and managing system administration and Azure resources.

R

Role-Based Access Control (RBAC)
A method of regulating access to computer or network resources based on roles assigned to individual users within an organization.

S

Scalability
The ability of a system or application to handle increased workloads by dynamically adding or removing resources.

Serverless Computing
Cloud computing model where cloud providers manage infrastructure, allowing developers to focus solely on code without server management tasks.

Software as a Service (SaaS)
Cloud-based software delivery model where applications are accessed over the internet rather than being locally installed.

T

Traffic Manager
An Azure service providing DNS-based traffic routing, optimizing user experience by distributing traffic based on geography, performance, or availability.

V

Virtual Machine (VM)
An emulation of a physical computer, providing similar functionality through virtualized hardware resources.

Common Acronyms

- **ARM** – Azure Resource Manager

- **CDN** – Content Delivery Network

- **CLI** – Command Line Interface

- **DNS** – Domain Name System

- **IaaS** – Infrastructure as a Service

- **IAM** – Identity and Access Management

- **JSON** – JavaScript Object Notation

- **PaaS** – Platform as a Service

- **RBAC** – Role-Based Access Control

- **REST** – Representational State Transfer

- **SaaS** – Software as a Service

- **SDK** – Software Development Kit

- **SLA** – Service Level Agreement

- **VM** – Virtual Machine

Code Examples for Key Terms:

Azure CLI Example: Creating a Resource Group

```
az group create --name MyResourceGroup --location eastus
```

PowerShell Example: Creating a Virtual Machine

```powershell
New-AzVm `
    -ResourceGroupName "MyResourceGroup" `
    -Name "MyVM" `
    -Location "East US" `
    -VirtualNetworkName "MyVnet" `
    -SubnetName "MySubnet" `
    -SecurityGroupName "MyNetworkSecurityGroup" `
    -PublicIpAddressName "MyPublicIP" `
    -OpenPorts 80,3389
```

ARM Template Example: Deploying a Storage Account

```json
{
  "$schema": "https://schema.management.azure.com/schemas/2019-04-01/deploymentTemplate.json#",
  "contentVersion": "1.0.0.0",
  "parameters": {
    "storageAccountType": {
      "type": "string",
      "defaultValue": "Standard_LRS"
    }
  },
  "resources": [
    {
      "type": "Microsoft.Storage/storageAccounts",
      "apiVersion": "2021-02-01",
      "name": "[concat('storage', uniqueString(resourceGroup().id))]",
      "location": "[resourceGroup().location]",
      "sku": {
        "name": "[parameters('storageAccountType')]"
      },
      "kind": "StorageV2",
      "properties": {}
    }
  ]
}
```

Final Notes:

This glossary provides a foundational understanding of key Azure concepts, terminology, and tools. Regularly consulting these definitions, along with practical application, enhances fluency and confidence when working within Azure's ecosystem. For further detailed descriptions and comprehensive coverage, refer to Microsoft's official Azure documentation, linked in subsequent appendices.

Resources for Further Learning

Expanding your knowledge of Microsoft Azure and cloud computing requires constant engagement with diverse learning materials. This section lists comprehensive resources, including official documentation, training platforms, online communities, video tutorials, books, and practical workshops. Each category provides valuable pathways for learners at every level.

Official Microsoft Resources

Microsoft offers extensive, regularly updated documentation designed to cover nearly every aspect of Azure development, deployment, and administration.

- **Microsoft Learn**
  Microsoft's primary educational platform providing free, interactive, and practical modules tailored to various roles, including developers, administrators, and architects.
  https://learn.microsoft.com/azure

- **Azure Documentation**
  The authoritative guide to Azure services and best practices, regularly maintained and updated with comprehensive tutorials, quick-start guides, API references, and example use-cases.
  https://docs.microsoft.com/azure

- **Azure Architecture Center**
  Detailed guidance for building secure, scalable, and optimized cloud architectures on Azure, including best practices, reference architectures, and solution ideas.
  https://docs.microsoft.com/azure/architecture

- **Azure Blog**
  Official announcements, feature updates, and case studies from Azure experts, Microsoft product teams, and community leaders.
  https://azure.microsoft.com/blog

- **Azure Roadmap**
  Stay ahead of upcoming Azure updates, features, and enhancements, including

timelines and planned changes across all Azure services.
https://azure.microsoft.com/updates

Certification and Training Platforms

Certifications offer structured learning pathways validated by industry-recognized exams, increasing employability and career opportunities.

- **Microsoft Certifications**
  Pathways for certifications like Azure Fundamentals (AZ-900), Azure Developer Associate (AZ-204), Azure Solutions Architect Expert (AZ-305), and more.
  https://learn.microsoft.com/certifications

- **Pluralsight**
  In-depth, structured courses and hands-on labs focused on Azure technologies, suitable for developers and architects looking for deep, technical training.
  https://www.pluralsight.com/paths/microsoft-azure-developer

- **Udemy**
  Offers extensive courses on Azure from beginner to expert, often with practical, project-based learning.
  https://www.udemy.com/topic/azure

- **Coursera**
  Provides Azure-related specializations and courses, often in collaboration with universities and leading technology companies.
  https://www.coursera.org/courses?query=azure

Books for Deep-Dive Learning

Books provide comprehensive insights into Azure, offering structured, detailed learning paths.

- **"Exam Ref AZ-204 Developing Solutions for Microsoft Azure" by Santiago Fernández Muñoz**
  Comprehensive preparation material for Azure Developer Associate certification, focused on practical applications and real-world scenarios.

- **"Azure for Architects" by Ritesh Modi**
  Designed for solutions architects aiming to build robust and scalable cloud solutions, covering extensive design patterns and best practices.

- **"Hands-On Azure for Developers" by Kamil Mrzygłód**
  Project-based book covering application development, deployment, and DevOps integration using Azure's tools and services.

- **"Learning Microsoft Azure Storage" by Mohamed Waly**
  Detailed examination of Azure's storage solutions, from basics to advanced scenarios involving performance tuning, data migration, and optimization.

- **"Microsoft Azure Security Infrastructure" by Yuri Diogenes and Nicholas DiCola**
  In-depth coverage of Azure's security features, compliance standards, and best practices for securing applications and infrastructure.

Community Forums and Discussion Groups

Online communities offer direct interaction with other Azure users, experts, and practitioners, allowing users to ask questions, solve problems, and share knowledge.

- **Microsoft Azure Community**
  Official forum providing direct assistance from Azure engineers, MVPs, and community members.
  https://learn.microsoft.com/answers/topics/azure.html

- **Stack Overflow – Azure**
  A vast community of developers who actively discuss, troubleshoot, and share solutions to Azure-related issues.
  https://stackoverflow.com/questions/tagged/azure

- **Reddit – r/Azure**
  Active subreddit dedicated to Azure-related news, discussions, and questions. Ideal for both new and experienced users.
  https://www.reddit.com/r/Azure

- **Azure Dev Community**
  Regular meetups, virtual events, and local groups focused on Azure development, infrastructure, and networking.
  https://developer.microsoft.com/azure

Video Tutorials and Channels

Visual learning through video tutorials can be especially beneficial for hands-on demonstrations and clear explanations of complex topics.

- **Microsoft Azure YouTube Channel**
  Official channel featuring Azure updates, tutorials, webinars, and demonstrations from Microsoft experts.
  https://www.youtube.com/@Azure

- **Azure Fridays (Channel 9)**
  Short, weekly episodes exploring Azure's latest technologies, demonstrations, and

innovations, hosted by Scott Hanselman and guests.
https://azure.microsoft.com/resources/videos/azure-friday

- **freeCodeCamp – Azure Tutorials**
  Comprehensive, free video tutorials covering various Azure concepts, from beginner to advanced.
  https://www.youtube.com/@freecodecamp

- **PluralSight YouTube Channel**
  A collection of Azure-focused webinars, demos, and interviews discussing advanced Azure topics, architectures, and strategies.
  https://www.youtube.com/@Pluralsight

Practical Labs and Hands-On Workshops

Hands-on labs offer practical experience, helping reinforce theoretical knowledge with real-world scenarios and simulations.

- **Azure Hands-On Labs by Microsoft Learn**
  Guided interactive labs allowing learners to test and practice Azure features in sandbox environments.
  https://learn.microsoft.com/azure

- **GitHub Azure Samples**
  Collection of Microsoft-authored and community-shared code samples demonstrating practical implementations of Azure services.
  https://github.com/Azure-Samples

- **Whizlabs Azure Labs**
  Practice Azure services in real-time environments, structured around certification scenarios and specific Azure roles.
  https://www.whizlabs.com/microsoft-azure-certification

Staying Up-to-Date

Cloud technologies evolve rapidly. Regularly following reliable resources ensures continuous learning and awareness of latest trends.

- **Azure Weekly Newsletter**
  Curated news and updates from the Azure ecosystem, delivered directly to your inbox weekly.
  https://azureweekly.info

- **Azure Updates RSS Feed**
  Automated updates of newly released Azure features, deprecations, and important announcements.

https://azure.microsoft.com/updates/feed

- **Twitter – Official Azure Account**
  Real-time announcements, Azure news, and direct engagement with Azure experts.
  https://twitter.com/Azure

These resources provide thorough pathways for continual growth in Azure proficiency. Utilizing these regularly, learners can develop deeper understanding, achieve technical excellence, and significantly enhance their capabilities in cloud computing.

Sample Projects and Code Snippets

This section provides practical examples and detailed code snippets to reinforce concepts covered throughout the book. By exploring these sample projects, you'll gain hands-on experience and a clearer understanding of how Azure services integrate into real-world scenarios. Each project illustrates key Azure concepts, such as serverless computing, database integration, storage management, DevOps pipelines, and monitoring.

Building a Simple Web Application with Azure App Services

In this project, you'll create a basic web application and deploy it to Azure App Services, demonstrating key steps including app creation, deployment, and scaling.

Step-by-step Example:

Step 1: Create a Simple Node.js Web Application

First, initialize a Node.js project and create a basic Express server:

```
npm init -y
npm install express
```

Create a file named app.js:

```
const express = require('express');
const app = express();
const port = process.env.PORT || 3000;

app.get('/', (req, res) => {
  res.send('Hello from Azure App Services!');
});

app.listen(port, () => {
```

```
    console.log(`App listening on port ${port}`);
});
```

Step 2: Deploy to Azure App Service

Deploy using Azure CLI:

```
az webapp up --name MySimpleAzureApp --runtime "NODE:18LTS" --
location eastus
```

Your web app is now accessible at:
https://MySimpleAzureApp.azurewebsites.net

Serverless Chatbot Using Azure Functions

Azure Functions allows easy serverless computing. Below is a chatbot backend using Azure Functions triggered by HTTP requests.

Function Example (`index.js`):

```
module.exports = async function (context, req) {
    const message = req.query.message || (req.body &&
req.body.message);

    if (message) {
        const reply = generateReply(message);
        context.res = {
            status: 200,
            body: { reply }
        };
    } else {
        context.res = {
            status: 400,
            body: "Please pass a message in the request."
        };
    }
};

function generateReply(message) {
    if (message.includes('hello')) {
        return 'Hi there! How can I help you today?';
```

```
    } else if (message.includes('help')) {
        return 'I am here to help you with Azure!';
    } else {
        return 'I'm sorry, I don't understand that.';
    }
}
```

Deploy via Azure CLI:

```
func azure functionapp publish MyServerlessChatbot
```

Integrating Azure Cosmos DB with Node.js Application

Cosmos DB offers powerful NoSQL capabilities. Here is how to integrate Cosmos DB into a Node.js app.

Initialize Cosmos DB client:

```
npm install @azure/cosmos
```

database.js snippet:

```
const { CosmosClient } = require('@azure/cosmos');

const endpoint = "<COSMOS_DB_ENDPOINT>";
const key = "<COSMOS_DB_KEY>";

const client = new CosmosClient({ endpoint, key });
const databaseId = 'UserDatabase';
const containerId = 'UserContainer';

async function createUser(user) {
  const { database } = await client.databases.createIfNotExists({
id: databaseId });
  const { container } = await
database.containers.createIfNotExists({ id: containerId });

  const { resource: createdItem } = await
container.items.create(user);
  return createdItem;
}
```

```javascript
module.exports = { createUser };
```

Use in your application:

```javascript
const { createUser } = require('./database');

createUser({ id: '1', name: 'John Doe', email: 'john@example.com' })
  .then(user => console.log(`Created user: ${user.name}`))
  .catch(err => console.error(err));
```

Continuous Deployment (CI/CD) Pipeline with Azure DevOps

Automating deployments enhances productivity. Here's a basic Azure Pipeline YAML configuration example.

azure-pipelines.yml:

```yaml
trigger:
  branches:
    include:
      - main

pool:
  vmImage: 'ubuntu-latest'

steps:
- task: NodeTool@0
  inputs:
    versionSpec: '18.x'
  displayName: 'Install Node.js'

- script: |
    npm install
    npm run build
  displayName: 'Install dependencies and build'

- task: AzureWebApp@1
  inputs:
    azureSubscription: 'Your Azure Subscription'
    appType: webApp
```

```
    appName: 'MySimpleAzureApp'
    package: '$(System.DefaultWorkingDirectory)'
  displayName: 'Deploy to Azure Web App'
```

Real-Time Logging and Monitoring with Azure Application Insights

Azure Monitor and Application Insights help you analyze app performance and availability.

Integrate into Node.js app:

```
npm install applicationinsights
```

`app.js` **configuration snippet:**

```
const appInsights = require('applicationinsights');
appInsights.setup('<INSTRUMENTATION_KEY>').start();

const express = require('express');
const app = express();
const port = process.env.PORT || 3000;

app.get('/', (req, res) => {
  res.send('Monitoring with Application Insights');
});

app.listen(port, () => {
  console.log(`Server running on port ${port}`);
});
```

View telemetry data, usage statistics, and errors in the Azure portal under Application Insights resource.

Creating an Azure Storage Account with Azure CLI

This example shows creating a storage account and uploading a blob file:

Create storage account:

```
az storage account create \
  --name mystorageaccount2024 \
```

```
--resource-group myResourceGroup \
--location eastus \
--sku Standard_LRS
```

Upload blob file:

```
az storage container create --name mycontainer --account-name
mystorageaccount2024
az storage blob upload --container-name mycontainer --name
example.txt --file ./example.txt --account-name mystorageaccount2024
```

Auto-scaling Azure App Service

Ensure performance during high load with auto-scaling rules via Azure CLI:

```
az monitor autoscale create \
  --resource-group myResourceGroup \
  --resource MySimpleAzureApp \
  --resource-type Microsoft.Web/sites \
  --name autoscaleSetting \
  --min-count 1 \
  --max-count 5 \
  --count 1
```

Set CPU-based scaling rules:

```
az monitor autoscale rule create \
  --resource-group myResourceGroup \
  --autoscale-name autoscaleSetting \
  --condition "Percentage CPU > 70 avg 5m" \
  --scale out 1
```

Azure RBAC Implementation Example

Implement Role-Based Access Control (RBAC) effectively:

Assign Contributor Role via Azure CLI:

```
az role assignment create \
  --assignee user@example.com \
```

```
--role "Contributor" \
--resource-group myResourceGroup
```

Integrating Azure Cognitive Services – Text Analytics API

Perform sentiment analysis on user input:

Install dependencies:

```
npm install @azure/ai-text-analytics
```

`analyze.js`:

```
const { TextAnalyticsClient, AzureKeyCredential } =
require('@azure/ai-text-analytics');

const key = "<COGNITIVE_SERVICES_KEY>";
const endpoint = "<COGNITIVE_SERVICES_ENDPOINT>";

const client = new TextAnalyticsClient(endpoint, new
AzureKeyCredential(key));

async function analyzeSentiment(text) {
  const [result] = await client.analyzeSentiment([text]);
  return result.sentiment;
}

analyzeSentiment("Azure is fantastic!").then(sentiment => {
  console.log(`Sentiment: ${sentiment}`);
});
```

By exploring these sample projects, you can solidify your practical knowledge and expertise, enabling you to confidently build, deploy, and manage robust Azure solutions.

API Reference Guide

This API Reference Guide provides detailed explanations and examples for commonly used APIs and endpoints within the Microsoft Azure ecosystem. It serves as a quick reference for developers to understand available methods, required parameters, responses, and best practices for interacting programmatically with Azure services.

Azure App Service API

Azure App Service allows managing web applications through RESTful endpoints, enabling programmatic control for deploying, managing, and scaling web applications.

List Web Apps

Retrieve details of all web applications within a subscription.

Request:

```
GET
https://management.azure.com/subscriptions/{subscriptionId}/provider
s/Microsoft.Web/sites?api-version=2022-09-01
```

Example Response:

```json
{
  "value": [
    {
      "id":
"/subscriptions/{subscriptionId}/resourceGroups/myResourceGroup/prov
iders/Microsoft.Web/sites/MyWebApp",
      "name": "MyWebApp",
      "type": "Microsoft.Web/sites",
      "location": "East US",
      "properties": {
        "state": "Running",
        "hostNames": ["mywebapp.azurewebsites.net"],
        "repositorySiteName": "MyWebApp",
        "usageState": "Normal"
      }
    }
  ]
}
```

Azure Functions API

Azure Functions provide APIs to manage serverless function apps, allowing you to create, delete, invoke, or update functions.

Trigger HTTP Function

Invoke a specific Azure Function via HTTP.

Request:

```
POST
https://{functionAppName}.azurewebsites.net/api/{functionName}?code=
{functionKey}
Content-Type: application/json

{
  "name": "Azure"
}
```

Example Response:

```
{
  "message": "Hello, Azure!"
}
```

Azure Cosmos DB API

Azure Cosmos DB provides robust REST APIs to interact with NoSQL databases, allowing CRUD operations, query execution, and resource management.

Retrieve Document from Cosmos DB

Fetch a single document using REST.

Request:

```
GET
https://{cosmosAccount}.documents.azure.com/dbs/{databaseId}/colls/{
collectionId}/docs/{documentId}
x-ms-version: 2018-12-31
x-ms-date: {date}
Authorization: {authToken}
```

Example Response:

```
{
  "id": "user123",
  "name": "John Doe",
```

```
"email": "john@example.com",
"_rid": "sample-rid",
"_self": "dbs/sampledb/colls/users/docs/user123/",
"_etag": "\"00005c12-0000-0000-0000-5d6d2c210000\"",
"_attachments": "attachments/",
"_ts": 1617923017
}
```

Azure Storage API

Azure Storage services expose REST APIs to manage Blob storage, file shares, queues, and tables programmatically.

Upload Blob to Storage Account

Store a blob in a specified container.

Request:

```
PUT
https://{accountName}.blob.core.windows.net/{containerName}/{blobNam
e}
x-ms-date: {date}
x-ms-version: 2022-11-02
Authorization: {authToken}
Content-Type: text/plain

Hello Azure Blob Storage!
```

Response (Success):

```
HTTP/1.1 201 Created
ETag: "0x8D9123456A89BCD"
```

Azure Monitor API

Azure Monitor enables retrieving diagnostic and telemetry data to manage application performance and availability.

Query Application Insights Metrics

Fetch telemetry metrics from Application Insights.

Request:

```
GET
https://api.applicationinsights.io/v1/apps/{appId}/metrics/requests/
count?timespan=PT12H
x-api-key: {apiKey}
```

Example Response:

```
{
  "value": {
    "start": "2024-01-01T00:00:00Z",
    "end": "2024-01-01T12:00:00Z",
    "requests/count": {
      "sum": 2456
    }
  }
}
```

Azure Cognitive Services API

These APIs deliver advanced AI capabilities including text analytics, speech recognition, and computer vision.

Sentiment Analysis with Text Analytics

Analyze text sentiment programmatically.

Request:

```
POST https://{endpoint}/text/analytics/v3.1/sentiment
Ocp-Apim-Subscription-Key: {key}
Content-Type: application/json

{
  "documents": [
    {
      "id": "1",
      "text": "Azure is amazing!"
    }
  ]
```

```
}
```

Example Response:

```json
{
  "documents": [
    {
      "id": "1",
      "sentiment": "positive",
      "confidenceScores": {
        "positive": 0.99,
        "neutral": 0.01,
        "negative": 0.0
      }
    }
  ]
}
```

Azure Virtual Machines API

Manage virtual machines programmatically, including provisioning, configuration, and decommissioning.

Create a Virtual Machine

Request:

```
PUT
https://management.azure.com/subscriptions/{subscriptionId}/resource
Groups/{resourceGroup}/providers/Microsoft.Compute/virtualMachines/{
vmName}?api-version=2023-07-01
Content-Type: application/json
Authorization: Bearer {token}

{
  "location": "eastus",
  "properties": {
    "hardwareProfile": {
      "vmSize": "Standard_DS1_v2"
    },
    "osProfile": {
```

```
      "computerName": "{vmName}",
      "adminUsername": "{adminUser}",
      "adminPassword": "{adminPassword}"
    },
    "storageProfile": {
      "imageReference": {
        "publisher": "MicrosoftWindowsServer",
        "offer": "WindowsServer",
        "sku": "2019-Datacenter",
        "version": "latest"
      },
      "osDisk": {
        "createOption": "FromImage"
      }
    },
    "networkProfile": {
      "networkInterfaces": [
        {
          "id":
"/subscriptions/{subscriptionId}/resourceGroups/{resourceGroup}/prov
iders/Microsoft.Network/networkInterfaces/{nicName}"
        }
      ]
    }
  }
}
```

Azure Resource Manager (ARM) API

Azure Resource Manager APIs provide resource deployment, management, and
governance capabilities.

Deploy ARM Template

Request:

```
PUT
https://management.azure.com/subscriptions/{subscriptionId}/resource
groups/{resourceGroup}/providers/Microsoft.Resources/deployments/{de
ploymentName}?api-version=2023-07-01
Authorization: Bearer {token}
```

```
Content-Type: application/json

{
  "properties": {
    "mode": "Incremental",
    "templateLink": {
      "uri":
"https://storageaccount.blob.core.windows.net/templates/storage-
account.json"
    },
    "parameters": {
      "storageAccountName": {
        "value": "mystorage2024"
      }
    }
  }
}
```

Azure Role-Based Access Control (RBAC) API

Manage access permissions programmatically with RBAC APIs.

Assign Role to a User

Request:

```
PUT
https://management.azure.com/subscriptions/{subscriptionId}/resource
Groups/{resourceGroup}/providers/Microsoft.Authorization/roleAssignm
ents/{roleAssignmentId}?api-version=2022-04-01
Authorization: Bearer {token}
Content-Type: application/json

{
  "properties": {
    "roleDefinitionId":
"/subscriptions/{subscriptionId}/providers/Microsoft.Authorization/r
oleDefinitions/{roleDefinitionId}",
    "principalId": "{principalId}"
  }
}
```

By utilizing this comprehensive reference guide, developers can confidently interact with Azure APIs, automate management tasks, and integrate powerful Azure services into their solutions effectively.

Frequently Asked Questions

This section addresses common questions, concerns, and clarifications related to Microsoft Azure, providing clear, concise answers to help deepen your understanding of key concepts and best practices.

General Azure Questions

Q: What is Microsoft Azure?
A: Microsoft Azure is a cloud computing platform provided by Microsoft, offering a wide range of services including computing power, storage, databases, artificial intelligence (AI), and networking solutions. Azure helps businesses build, deploy, manage, and scale applications quickly without extensive hardware or infrastructure investments.

Q: How does Azure pricing work?
A: Azure pricing varies by service and usage. Pricing models include pay-as-you-go, reserved instances (long-term discounts), spot instances (discounted pricing for spare capacity), and hybrid benefits. Detailed pricing can be estimated using the Azure Pricing Calculator.

Q: Is Azure secure and compliant?
A: Azure complies with numerous global security standards, including ISO 27001, GDPR, HIPAA, and others. It offers robust security features such as Azure Security Center, Role-Based Access Control (RBAC), encryption at rest and in transit, and advanced threat protection.

Azure Development Questions

Q: What's the difference between Azure App Service and Azure Functions?
A: Azure App Service provides a fully managed platform to deploy web and mobile applications, ideal for continuous-running apps. Azure Functions, in contrast, offer serverless computing, designed to run event-driven code without managing infrastructure, suitable for microservices and automation tasks.

Q: How do I set up continuous deployment (CI/CD) in Azure?
A: You can use Azure DevOps or GitHub Actions to set up CI/CD pipelines. A typical pipeline includes steps to build, test, and deploy your application automatically from a repository to Azure services. Azure DevOps provides comprehensive pipeline management, and YAML-based configurations offer easy customization.

Example (Azure DevOps Pipeline YAML):

```yaml
trigger:
  branches:
    include:
      - main

pool:
  vmImage: 'ubuntu-latest'

steps:
  - script: npm install && npm test
    displayName: 'Install dependencies and run tests'

  - task: AzureWebApp@1
    inputs:
      azureSubscription: 'YourSubscription'
      appName: 'YourWebAppName'
      package: '$(System.DefaultWorkingDirectory)'
    displayName: 'Deploy to Azure Web App'
```

Azure Storage and Database Questions

Q: When should I use Cosmos DB vs. Azure SQL Database?
A: Use Cosmos DB for flexible NoSQL applications that require rapid scaling, global replication, and schema flexibility. Azure SQL Database is suitable for relational data models, complex queries, structured transactions, and applications leveraging traditional SQL features.

Q: How do I back up my Azure databases?
A: Azure databases provide automated backup features. For Azure SQL Database, automated backups are stored for 7 to 35 days. Cosmos DB offers continuous backups and point-in-time restore. Additionally, manual backups can be managed through Azure CLI or PowerShell.

Example (manual Azure SQL backup):

```sql
CREATE DATABASE YourDBCopy AS COPY OF YourDatabase;
```

Azure Resource Management Questions

Q: What is Azure Resource Manager (ARM)?
 A: Azure Resource Manager is a management layer enabling you to deploy, manage, and organize Azure resources using declarative templates (ARM templates), CLI, PowerShell, or REST APIs, ensuring consistent deployment and management across Azure environments.

Q: How do I create resources using ARM templates?
 A: Resources can be created using JSON-formatted ARM templates defining resources and configurations, then deployed via the Azure portal, CLI, or Azure DevOps.

Example (ARM template snippet):

```
{
  "$schema": "https://schema.management.azure.com/schemas/2019-04-
01/deploymentTemplate.json#",
  "contentVersion": "1.0.0.0",
  "resources": [
    {
      "type": "Microsoft.Storage/storageAccounts",
      "name": "mystorage2024",
      "apiVersion": "2021-09-01",
      "location": "[resourceGroup().location]",
      "sku": {
        "name": "Standard_LRS"
      },
      "kind": "StorageV2",
      "properties": {}
    }
  ]
}
```

Azure Security Questions

Q: How can I secure my Azure resources?
 A: Secure Azure resources by implementing best practices like:

- Role-Based Access Control (RBAC)

- Multi-factor authentication (MFA) using Azure AD

- Regular audits and monitoring via Azure Security Center

- Encryption of data at rest and in transit

- Network security groups and firewalls

Q: What is Azure Security Center?
A: Azure Security Center provides unified security management, monitoring, and threat protection across Azure resources. It helps detect threats, provides security recommendations, manages security policies, and ensures compliance.

Azure Scalability Questions

Q: How do I auto-scale Azure services?
A: Azure services like App Service, Functions, and Virtual Machines can auto-scale based on metrics such as CPU utilization, memory consumption, or request rates, configurable via Azure Monitor autoscale settings.

Example (Azure CLI auto-scale configuration):

```
az monitor autoscale create \
  --resource-group MyResourceGroup \
  --resource MyAppService \
  --resource-type Microsoft.Web/sites \
  --name MyAutoscaleSetting \
  --min-count 1 --max-count 5 --count 1

az monitor autoscale rule create \
  --resource-group MyResourceGroup \
  --autoscale-name MyAutoscaleSetting \
  --condition "Percentage CPU > 70 avg 5m" \
  --scale out 1
```

Azure Cost Management Questions

Q: How do I control my Azure spending?
A: Control Azure costs through:

- Setting budgets and alerts with Azure Cost Management

- Monitoring resource usage regularly

- Selecting appropriate resource sizes and pricing tiers

- Using Azure Reservations or spot instances

- Eliminating unused or idle resources regularly

Q: What are Azure Reservations?
 A: Azure Reservations allow you to reserve resources like Virtual Machines or SQL databases in advance at discounted rates for 1 or 3 years, significantly reducing costs compared to pay-as-you-go.

Azure Certification Questions

Q: Which Azure certification should I pursue first?
 A: The Azure Fundamentals (AZ-900) certification is ideal for beginners, providing a foundational understanding of cloud concepts, services, security, and pricing. For developers, Azure Developer Associate (AZ-204) is recommended.

Q: How can I prepare for Azure certification exams?
 A: Preparation steps include:

- Completing learning paths on Microsoft Learn

- Practicing hands-on labs and sample projects

- Reviewing official documentation thoroughly

- Taking practice exams online (MeasureUp, Whizlabs)

Azure Support Questions

Q: Where can I get help with Azure issues?
 A: For support, consider:

- Azure Support via Azure Portal (raising tickets)

- Microsoft Q&A Forums (learn.microsoft.com)

- Stack Overflow for developer-related queries

- Community forums like Reddit (r/Azure)

This extensive FAQ section serves as a quick-reference resource for troubleshooting common issues, clarifying essential concepts, and enhancing your proficiency in working effectively with Microsoft Azure.

www.ingramcontent.com/pod-product-compliance
Lightning Source LLC
LaVergne TN
LVHW051432050326
832903LV00030BD/3047